THE WALRUS & THE ELEPHANTS

JOHN LENNON'S YEARS OF REVOLUTION

JAMES A. MITCHELL

SEVEN STORIES PRESS
New York

Seven Stories Press
140 Watts Street
New York, NY 10013
www.sevenstories.com

College professors may request free examination copies of Seven Stories Press titles. To order, visit http://www.sevenstories.com/textbook or send a fax on school letterhead to (212) 226-1411.

Book design by Stewart Cauley Design and Elizabeth DeLong

Library of Congress Cataloging-in-Publication Data

Mitchell, James.
  The walrus and the elephants : John Lennon's years of revolution / James Mitchell. -- First edition.
    pages cm
  ISBN 978-1-60980-467-1 (hardcover)
  1. Lennon, John, 1940-1980. 2. Rock musicians--England--Biography. I. Title.
  ML420.L38J36 2013
  782.42166092--dc23
  [B]
                    2013017514

Printed in the United States

9 8 7 6 5 4 3 2 1

Contents

To the memory of Wayne "Tex" Gabriel—a gifted musician and a good man.

And to the spirit of John Lennon, of whom many have said the same thing.

"Was he jailed for what he'd done, or representing everyone?"
—John Lennon,
"John Sinclair"

CHAPTER ONE

THE ADVENT OF THE HIPPIE MESSIAH

"We came here . . . not only to help John and to spotlight what's going on . . . but also to show and to say to all of you that apathy isn't it, and that we can do something."
—JOHN LENNON
(Ann Arbor, MI, December 1971)

IN DECEMBER 1971 John Lennon stood onstage to sing and speak on behalf of John Sinclair, a radical leader who was serving a ten-year prison sentence for possession of two joints of marijuana. Sinclair had been incarcerated for more than two years when Lennon pleaded his case.

Two days after Lennon sang, "Let him be, set him free," a state circuit court reversed a previous decision and Sinclair walked out of prison.

With the nation reeling after years of political turmoil,

America needed a new kind of leader. The recently turned ex-Beatle was one of the most famous and influential people on the planet. If he could get a man out of prison, what else might he do?

A government eager to silence enemies asked the same question. They thought Lennon might use his considerable clout to, in their words, "sway" the upcoming presidential election. It would be better for some people if he just went back to England, and the Nixon administration tried to make that happen through methods legal and otherwise.

"So flower power didn't work," Lennon said from the stage between songs that night. "So what? We start again."

•   •   •

JOHN LENNON FELT like a newcomer to New York in the summer of 1971. He'd been to the city before, of course, but those were whirlwind Beatles visits, frantic tours where Manhattan was seen from limousines and hotel rooms. Lennon sought a lower-profile life, ironically in the very place where, seven years earlier, he had launched the "British invasion" of English rock and everything that followed. Back then all it took was an electric guitar, a smart-ass grin, and "Yeah, yeah, yeah."

But this time there were no teenage screams to drown out the music, no mobs of girls desperate for a glimpse at a Beatle. It wasn't the sixties anymore, a decade of war and assassinations, flower power and protests. Lennon was no longer one of the "Fab Four," a point he made often.

"Tried to shake our image just a cycling through the Village," Lennon wrote in "New York City," among a fresh batch of songs inspired by his new home. He and wife Yoko Ono had stayed first in Midtown's St. Regis hotel before settling that fall at 105 Bank Street on the west side of Greenwich Village, a space formerly occupied by drummer Joe Butler of the Lovin' Spoonful.[1] The downtown neighborhood suited Lennon's frame of mind: a gritty yet colorful free-for-all of music, radical politics, art, and dope smoked openly on the streets; an atmosphere worthy of the finest psychedelic "Sgt. Pepper" vibes.

The apartment was modest by New York standards, barely two rooms more functional than spacious. It was worlds apart from Tittenhurst, the English estate Lennon left behind, a home that made an ironic setting in the eyes of more than a few critics of the *Imagine* promotional film ("imagine no possessions"). Lennon was apparently embarrassed by his wealth, among other by-products of Beatlemania. He told authors Peter McCabe and Robert Schonfield, who that summer had been researching a book on the Beatles' breakup, *Apple to the Core*, "I can't really go on the road and take a lot more money. What am I going to do with it? I've got all the fucking bread I need."[2]

It wasn't a random thought; he'd recently discussed the "Imagine" lyrics with Hendrik Hertzberg of the *New Yorker*.[3] "I began to think: I don't want that big house we built for ourselves in England," Lennon acknowledged. "I don't want the bother of owning all those big houses and big cars. It's clogging my mind just to think about what amount of gear I have in England. All my books and possessions; walls full of books I've collected."

Lennon thought those books belonged elsewhere, in libraries and prisons, as with most of his other belongings.

Lennon was trying to get away from the trappings of wealth and fame, and with equal intensity longed to take part in something larger than himself and bigger than the Beatles, if that could be imagined. The explosive political and cultural conflicts that had been brewing in America demanded his attention. In early 1971, Lennon had given extensive interviews to *Rolling Stone* and *Red Mole*, a British underground newspaper edited by Tariq Ali. Lennon was "ashamed" that he hadn't been more active in antiwar and civil rights movements. He had often felt torn between the commercialism of early Beatles success—"everybody trying to use us"—and the desire to sneak more adult topics into their songs: "We'd turned out to be a Trojan horse."[4]

He had been cautious, though, understandably hesitant after enduring media scrutiny and public backlash on more than one occasion. There had been legendary scandals including his taken-out-of-context, blown-out-of-proportion observation that British youth weren't too keen on the church and that the Beatles were more popular than Jesus Himself. He told Ali that, back in those days, manager Brian Epstein begged the boys not to weigh in on what had become the dominant issue in America.

"Epstein tried to waffle on at us about saying nothing about Vietnam," Lennon explained. "George and I said, 'Listen, when they ask next time, we're going to say we don't like the war and we think they should get right out.' . . . That was a pretty radical thing to do, especially for the 'Fab Four.'"

There were, at the time, internal differences of opinion about the Beatles' place in the world as artistic or revolutionary leaders. Before leaving England Lennon had exchanged letters with Paul and Linda McCartney, prompted by public statements regarding the group's legacy. "Do you really think most of today's art came about because of the Beatles?" Lennon asked. "I'm not ashamed of the Beatles—(I did start it all)."[5]

He also wanted to keep their achievements in perspective: "Didn't we always say we were part of the Movement—not all of it? Of course we changed the world—but try and follow it through—GET OFF YOUR GOLD DISC AND FLY!"

Lennon and McCartney realized that more involvement had been expected of them as a group. *Red Mole* publisher Ali, an Indian-born, British-raised journalist who was among the new breed of counterculture scribes, had written that artists of Lennon's stature had an obligation to do more than just flash an occasional peace sign. At the same time, Lennon hadn't fully come to terms with his newfound revolutionary status.

"He was very modest about it," recalls Ali. "He said, 'Are you sure you want to do an interview with me? Your magazine is so intellectual.'"

For the better part of two days they discussed Vietnam, politics, activism, and the challenges the '60s generation now faced.

"It was John Lennon's 'State of the Union' message," Ali says. "That's what it was to the world at that point in time."

Lennon wanted to be involved, and had been among the first to admit that the youth culture of the sixties had perhaps been a bit too laid-back in its approach.

"The acid dream is over," Lennon said. "That's what I'm trying

to tell them." As a musician he could offer songs that brought
people together, like the 1969 anthem "Give Peace a Chance,"
written and recorded during a very public honeymoon spent
on bedded display before the world's cameras. He envisioned
that the song could be sung "in the pub or on a demonstration."
He took it a step further in 1971 with "Power to the People," and
told Ali that his post-Beatles plans included a more active role
in the Movement: "I would like to compose songs for the revolution. . . . I hope they see that rock and roll is not the same as
Coca-Cola. That's why I'm putting out more heavy statements
now and trying to shake off the teeny-bopper image."[6]

In America Lennon was ready to practice what he preached.
"Get on your feet," Lennon said in "Power to the People," and
"into the street." He loved the idea that he could, more or less,
freely walk around Manhattan just like everyone else. The
city was alive; the Village a heartbeat that measured the pulse
of the streets. Lennon felt it in the basement hangouts of St.
Marks Place, the bars on Bleecker, and in Washington Square
Park, where the central fountain was a magnet for struggling
musicians with talent ranging from up-and-coming to proba-
bly-not-happening but no less passionate. John and Yoko casually joined the crowds who enjoyed music played for its own
sake, songs not likely to be heard on Top 10 radio.

"Up come a man with a guitar in his hand singing, 'Have a
marijuana if you can.'" David Peel and his Lower East Side band,
as immortalized in Lennon's "New York City," were among the
park's regular acts, singing and playing for fun and whatever
spare change people tossed into an open guitar case. Pot featured

prominently in Peel compositions, earnest songs about street life and being a hippie in the city.

In spite of Peel's amateur abilities, Lennon was taken by the music. The songs were of, by, and for the people, and to Lennon's ears seemed far more intimate, more relevant than the inherently commercial nature of popular music. Being too successful wasn't necessarily considered cool in the Village.

"Why do we have to pay to see stars?" Peel asked his audience, a rhetorical question from the perspective of a struggling musician.[7]

"He must be talking about me," Lennon reportedly mused. He'd been wrestling with the very nature of being a pop star just as he had his standing in the revolutionary world.

•   •   •

IN WASHINGTON SQUARE Park Lennon first met Jerry Rubin, a friend of Peel's and one of the "Chicago Seven" defendants who, three years earlier, had been charged with inciting riots at the 1968 Democratic Convention.

Lennon said that upon arriving in New York, "the first people who got in touch with me were Jerry Rubin and Abbie Hoffman. It's as simple as that."[8]

Lennon seemed the answer to the radical leaders' long-mumbled prayers; it was "love at first sight" from Rubin's perspective. "Great vibes," Rubin described the meeting, confident that Lennon shared his vision. "The Yippies had been applying Beatles tactics to politics, trying to merge music and life."

The Youth International Party—the "Yippies"—were an informal group of antiwar and civil rights activists fronted by Rubin and Hoffman. In Chicago they had joined forces with New Left leaders including Rennie Davis and Tom Hayden. Their Chicago activities made them famous in some circles, notorious in others. Supporters who gave trial testimony on behalf of all the Chicago defendants included Judy Collins, Arlo Guthrie, Norman Mailer, Timothy Leary, Reverend Jesse Jackson, and others, but the 1970 court proceedings were mostly seen as a media circus dominated by Hoffman and Rubin's absurdist theater tactics. Among other stunts, they wore judicial robes to court one day, underneath which—certain they'd be ordered to remove the garments—were Chicago Police Department uniforms. The Seven had been found guilty of crossing state lines to start a riot, and lived with a suspended sentence hanging over their heads for two years before being acquitted.

The Chicago Seven—Rubin, Hoffman, Davis, Dave Dellinger, Hayden, John Froines, and Lee Weiner—had followed separate paths since the trial; some as de facto leaders of the antiwar movement, others as media-fueled celebrities. By 1971 Hoffman and Rubin's act may have worn thin: ABC News dismissed them as "Groucho Marxists," not to be taken seriously given their street-theater gags like a mock campaign to elect a pig president (Pigasus the Immortal) or throwing money onto the floor of the stock exchange for a laugh. Davis says there was essentially a schism on the Left around the effectiveness of Hoffman and Rubin, and a guiding force was needed if they were to reenergize in time to replace Nixon as president.

Maybe it was only the end of a difficult decade, but the nation's spirit of rebellion seemed broken. Many activists continued their work, but on a local level—in schools and communities rather than on the international stage of the antiwar movement. *Time* magazine wondered if the dreaded bomb of student protest was a dud. "Something has happened in American life—or has failed to happen," offered a February essay entitled "The Cooling of America": "In dead winter, 1971, after months of recession, a decade of war abroad and domestic violence, a mood approaching quiet has fallen like a deep snow."

"There was so much steam to oppose the war," says Davis, a Michigan native who cut his revolutionary teeth in Ann Arbor. "The steam ran out. Everybody could see it; you couldn't get anybody to do anything."

Davis recalls reading John Lennon's revolution-fueled interviews and recognizing not just a kindred spirit, but one who could revitalize a fading antiwar movement.

"It was an extraordinary moment to me," Davis says. "Here was this human being, who symbolized so well his entire generation through the Beatles, making statements that clearly indicated he was not just saying, 'I'm for peace.' This was someone saying, 'I'm an activist, I'm ready to join up.'"

Lennon landed in America at a precarious time, a time when thousands were being arrested, when a few protesters had been killed, and when thousands were dying in Vietnam. So you didn't necessarily hang back. You put yourself on the line. You made a statement of your active involvement. Lennon had never considered himself a political man, but maybe times had changed. In an October interview with the underground *Los Angeles Free Press*, Lennon said he'd only recently understood what he might have to offer.

"I wouldn't say I've given up politics in that way," Lennon reflected.[9] "I mean, I never took up politics. Things I do—or for that matter anybody does—are done politically. Any statement you make is a political statement. Any record, even your way of life is a political statement."

The Movement too was at a crossroads: Was the spirit and passion that had begun with the civil rights movement nearing an end? Davis waxed nostalgic for the sheer rightness of the struggle as it had been, that had begun when four black students sat at a Woolworth's diner reserved for "whites only" and inspired a six-month boycott of the store . . . and for the decade that had followed.

"It was clear to everyone, especially myself, that this enormous thing that began in 1960 at a lunch counter in Greensboro, North Carolina, was now a phenomenon, a historic event," Davis says. "And now, clearly, it was ending."

Or was it? In John Lennon, Davis and Rubin saw a glimpse of hope. Rubin needed something to restore his credibility, not only with mainstream America but within the Movement itself. In some ways, Rubin faced similar life issues to Lennon's—concerned about his future and uncertain of the legacy he'd thus far written. Rubin told *Rolling Stone* that he had more than a few doubts about his—and the revolution's—future.[10]

"Everyone around me was depressed and confused," Rubin said. "Everyone in the Movement was condemning everything . . . condemning our whole history."

Lennon in New York presented a rare opportunity that Rubin eagerly seized. He placed a shot-in-the-dark call to Apple

Records and was as surprised as anyone when Yoko called him back. Rubin and Hoffman's first encounter with John and Yoko fittingly took place beneath Washington Square's landmark arch; Lennon wore American flag sneakers, Yoko was all in black. After excited introductions they left the park and spent several hours in Hoffman's apartment. Rubin told John and Yoko that their bed-ins for peace were great, not unlike his own political stunts. John and Yoko said they considered Hoffman and Rubin to be artists; the radical leaders saw Lennon as a new kind of political activist.

Rubin asked early and often what exactly Lennon wanted to do. To be involved, Lennon told him. He wanted to put a band together, play music, and "give all the money back to the people"; to use his music and do his part for the Movement. He had said he intended to "compose songs for the revolution," and hoped to take those songs on the road and maybe shake things up a little.

"I want to do something political, and radicalize people and all that jazz," Lennon said. "This would be the best way . . . taking a really far-out show on the road, a mobile, political rock and roll show."

If he'd been back in London Lennon would have had all the contacts he wanted, as he dipped a tentative toe in British revolutionary waters, but in America he required some introductions to find the right causes to rally. Rubin's usefulness relied on whether the Yippie leader could serve as Lennon's tour guide into Left politics, Yankee style. He had to bring something to the Bank Street party to stand out from the dreamers and schemers who sought Lennon's friendship, confidence, and favors.

A specific issue piqued Lennon's interest, the struggles of
Rubin's friend, Detroit activist John Sinclair, who was serving a
harsh prison sentence: ten years for marijuana possession that
instead seemed like punishment for his political views.

Either the sales pitch or the cause—ten years for two lousy
joints!—clinched the deal. The immediacy of the effort appealed
to Lennon—grab a guitar, fly to Michigan, and get involved, and
for the crowd to do more than just scream in delight.

"We want the audience to participate fully, and not just admire
God onstage," Lennon told French TV reporter Jean-François
Vallee, who spent a day filming a Bank Street bed-chat with John,
Yoko, and Rubin in early December.[11] Lennon described the vision
he'd been forming of a politically charged concert, free of super-
star trappings, with the people and performers united in spirit.

That seemed to have been the problem when the Beatles last
tried to perform in front of a crowd—and who knew what might
happen if all four took the stage together again. "I am still mainly a
musician," Lennon said, perhaps wistfully, as he prepared to begin
a new chapter in his career. Partly, his goal was to be just another
musician, one without the superstar trappings; at the same time,
in his writing and performing he was seeking to shine as an artist
in ways that might even surpass what he had accomplished as a
member of a group, even if the group did happen to be the Beatles.

"As an individual I still have a lot of power, I can always get on
the media . . . because of the Beatles," Lennon said. "Our job now is
to tell them there is still hope and we still have things to do and we
must get out now and change their heads. We can change! It isn't
over just because flower power didn't work. It's only the beginning."

Lennon thought he'd found exactly what he'd hoped for when he left Britain, a chance to serve the Movement with his guitar and presence.

•   •   •

LENNON MAY HAVE been John Sinclair's last hope for getting out of prison. Two years into his sentence and nothing had worked, not letter-writing campaigns to the *Detroit News* or *Free Press*, not even when Abbie Hoffman tried to take the stage at Woodstock and say a few words about Sinclair's ordeal. (Abbie's timing was off: he stepped onstage while the Who were doing their thing, and legend holds that guitarist Pete Townshend belted Hoffman with his Gibson and sent him off.)

Sinclair was an underground Detroit legend dating back to his Wayne State University days in the early 1960s. A man of eclectic tastes in addition to an affinity for weed, Sinclair composed poetry, advocated for political causes and community benefits, and promoted his beloved jazz. With his future wife, German-born Magdalene "Leni" Arndt, Sinclair transformed the 1964-launched Detroit Artists Workshop into the more political, civil rights–driven White Panther Party, a name taken in response to Black Panther Huey Newton's call to arms to people of all colors. Although the name was potentially confusing (and later changed to the Rainbow People's Party), the White Panthers sympathized with what they considered a natural ally in the wake of the 1967 riots that rocked the Motor City.

"The hippies and the black people had the same enemy: the Detroit Police Department," Sinclair says. "Another common bond was we smoked weed and so did most of them. Certainly the ones we came in contact with, artists and poets."

Whether hippie or Panther, Sinclair said they shared common bonds as easily distinguishable minorities in a country divided by a so-called generation gap.

"They had a sign: long hair," Sinclair says. "If you had long hair, smoked dope, liked rock and roll, didn't have a job, and liked to fuck, you were a hippie. Hippies were great; best thing to ever happen to this country."

Sinclair's casual demeanor, that of the frequently if not perpetually stoned, could be deceptive; he was passionate and focused on the issues he championed. From a core of community-based idealism, his grassroots efforts tackled causes large and small but always local, unlike the higher-profile activists who basked in the national spotlight. While sympathetic, Sinclair pointed out that Detroit had its own problems.

"We were totally outside the established realm of politics, of which the left wing was the SDS and the mobilization of all the antiwar stuff," Sinclair says. "We were always in support of that, but we were coming from a different cultural perspective."

The local attention—good and bad—was just as intense as the national scrutiny faced by Rubin and Hoffman. Sinclair's passions for pot and politics made him a target for campus police who considered longhairs enemies of the state.

"I was busted twice before," Sinclair recalls. "Once for selling a ten-dollar 'matchbox' to an undercover police officer; the second time an undercover policeman induced me to drive him to someone's house where I got him a ten-dollar bag."

The second arrest in 1965 ended with Sinclair spending six months in the Detroit House of Corrections. What should have been a cautionary tale—quit giving pot to relative strangers—didn't take hold. Back on the streets, Sinclair continued his laid-back approach to freely sharing the weed.

"We were hippies, you know, we weren't criminals," he says. "We didn't consider ourselves engaged in criminal behavior. Everything we did was open, free to the public, that's what we were about."

Everyone was welcome at the Detroit Artists Workshop, including two newcomers in late 1966: a man with long hair and a beret called "Louie," and a woman introduced as "Pat" who wore hippie clothes, smoked pot, and helped with the typing.[12] Pat played up to the men and Louie tried to score pot from whomever he could. Louie and Pat—in reality Vahan Kapagian and Jane Mumford of the Detroit Police Department—were comfortable with the hippies, and one memorable day Pat asked a question often heard at the workshop.

"She asked me if I had a joint," Sinclair says. "I rolled a joint, we had a smoke. She asked if she could take it with her. I said, 'Here, let me give you another one,' so I gave her a second one."

The word "entrapment" probably didn't slow down the two officers who, a month later, stormed the workshop with some of their friends and a fistful of warrants. Sinclair was arrested along with fifty-five others in what the papers called a "campus dope raid." The charges dragged through two years' worth of appeals, and in 1969 Sinclair began a ten-year prison sentence for a pair of joints.

For two years his friends and supporters had tried everything they could think of—appeals to sympathetic lawmakers, letters and advertisements in newspapers—but Sinclair remained stuck in prison. Hope came in two forms. The first was a political gambit played in July 1971 by President Richard Nixon when he lowered the voting age from twenty-one to eighteen. The impact went well beyond the election of the president; candidates at all levels of government would now need to sell their platforms to a generation that they had barely acknowledged before, let alone understood. Of particular interest to the college crowd, the politicians would quickly learn, were laws criminalizing marijuana use. Legislators across the country weighed whether it might be time to reduce simple possession from a felony to a misdemeanor.

Sinclair's supporters hoped this might be the chance they'd been waiting for to get Sinclair's story back in the public spotlight, told on front pages and evening newscasts. Sometimes it took sensational efforts, something as loud as a Yippie stunt, but backed up by mainstream credibility. A concert to rally the pro-pot, antiwar crowd could be the perfect combustion of audience and cause—if the right acts could be found. They needed a big star to draw the right amount of attention.

"We were always reaching for more," Sinclair says. "This time we hit the jackpot."

•   •   •

CONCERT PROMOTER PETER Andrews didn't believe it was really happening until John Lennon answered the phone.

Andrews and Leni Sinclair had flown to New York equipped with little more than a Jerry Rubin–provided phone number and some downtown addresses.

Andrews was well experienced in booking concerts in Ann Arbor, everything from local acts to Jefferson Airplane. He'd been approached about the intimidating task of filling the fifteen-thousand-seat Crisler Arena on behalf of a jailed poet.

"Sinclair wanted a big event," Andrews says. "He's in jail telling folks, 'I need something big here.'"

What they had wasn't enough. Andrews says the original plans for the Ann Arbor show included local musicians and a host of speakers, which might fill three thousand seats at best and leave a sad, empty-looking arena. Besides, wasn't John Sinclair old news?

"I looked at what they had and said, 'You have a real bomb on your hands,'" Andrews recalls. "He'd been in prison two years, and people have short memories."

Andrews considered the idea without much enthusiasm, until Leni Sinclair relayed an intriguing offer: John Lennon and Yoko Ono as headliners.

No way, thought Andrews. "It was too far out," he says. "The idea of him performing was pretty outrageous."

But it was real, and soon it was happening. Andrews and Leni shook their heads at their good fortune and set about closing the deal. While Andrews headed for Bank Street to confirm Lennon's interest in the concert, Leni took a cab to Jerry Rubin's Prince Street apartment to discuss adding another top-shelf artist to the line-up. Braced against the December chill she rang the bell. Hearing no response, Leni waited on the stoop for him to return.

"Before long, a man came up and rang the same doorbell," Leni says. He, too, was there to see Rubin, and they had a brief conversation. Leni told the kindred spirit of her husband's plight and how Rubin and John Lennon planned to help. Another man soon approached who had a key to the building, and they went inside to wait for Rubin.

"I sat in a chair and these two gentlemen started a conversation," Leni says. "I'm listening out of one ear, and it dawns on me that it was Bob Dylan and Phil Ochs. Jerry Rubin was trying to get Bob Dylan to play this concert with John Lennon."

A true radical dating back to when she fled Germany and dove headlong into Detroit's underground scene, Leni felt somewhat out of her league when she realized the company she was in.

"I never saw them again, and he didn't do the concert," Leni says. I don't hold that against him—you don't need Bob Dylan if you've got John Lennon." And though Dylan didn't end up on the bill for the Michigan concert, Phil Ochs did.

The trip from Detroit was an unqualified if unbelievable success: one of the world's most sought-after performers was set to champion the Sinclair cause. Andrews had a signed contract that paid Lennon $500 for his performance, a fee immediately signed back over to the John Sinclair Freedom Fund.[13] The fee-turned-donation was a paltry sum, of course, and Lennon was well aware that the many groups and activists who sought him out did so in part from financial need.

"I always take care of the underground," Lennon had said a

few months earlier. He also had his own vision of what charity or benefits could accomplish. "If they get in trouble I lend them money or invest in them or whatever. I get asked every two days for at least five thousand pounds, and I usually give it to them."[14] Lennon had in mind a foundation built on "a dollar a head" concert receipts that could benefit those who came calling.

Of equal value was Lennon the performer, and the musical stamp of incalculable worth he could put on a given cause. With Sinclair in mind, Lennon previewed a song he'd started writing for the occasion, a bluesy number strummed on a steel guitar.

"I assured him it was very good," Andrews says. "And that John Sinclair would indeed love it."

Andrews, stunned at the prospect of a John Lennon concert, humbly asked Lennon to say a few words into a tape recorder, an oral testament to confirm the contents of the hastily drawn-up contract.[15] Lennon's message was brief, to the point, even semi-apologetic in some ways:

> *This is John and I'm with Yoko here. I just want to say we're coming along to the John Sinclair bust fund or rally or whatever it is to say hello. I won't be bringing a band or nothing like that because I'm only here as a tourist, but I'll probably fetch me guitar and we have a song that we wrote for John. That's that. We'll be there Friday . . . hello and goodbye and hope that's fine.*

•   •   •

NATURALLY, JOHN LENNON and Yoko Ono were treated like royalty when they arrived in Michigan on Friday, December 10. Andrews booked—ironically—the presidential suite of Ann Arbor's Campus Inn, where he brought the couple after picking them up at the airport.

Selling tickets with Lennon's name on the bill was hardly a concern—the three-dollar entry fee was remarkably low even by 1971 standards—and the show sold out within a few hours. Andrews said that the modest price was at Sinclair's insistence, a "for the people" philosophy he later regretted.

"We had a breakeven budget and nobody got paid," Andrews says. "I wanted to charge twenty bucks, gross $300,000, and we'd sell out in the same amount of time. You don't get too many opportunities to present John Lennon."

As in New York, Lennon hoped to downplay his fame, to be one of the street people in the college town's hip stores and bustling downtown. Lennon spent part of the afternoon wandering through the shops, including some time with star-struck musicians in the Herb David Guitar Studio at the corner of Liberty and Fourth Street. There was no fanfare, owner David told the *Ann Arbor Chronicle*; Lennon simply walked in, so unassuming that at first he wasn't recognized by some of the people in the store.[16]

The owner knew perfectly well who was standing in his shop. "Hi John," David said before introducing himself.

"I'm not John. I'm his cousin," Lennon grinned in response.

"Hello cousin," David smiled back, and invited Lennon to relax and sit in a simple wooden chair. Lennon spent more than an hour in the store, at one point playing guitar to the delight of stunned customers. (The chair remained in place four decades later. A cardboard sign read, *John Lennon sat here in 1971*, a museum-worthy piece revered like presidential memorabilia.)

By evening Lennon was backstage at Crisler, where he patiently showed guitar chords to his improvised band. Satisfied that his support group understood the songs as well as could be reasonably expected, Lennon waited to close the show.

It was a long wait. The program began shortly after seven p.m. with the poet Allen Ginsberg, whose ballad of Sinclair had been given to Lennon as background information on the cause. It seemed a joint was lit each time John Sinclair's name was invoked, as smoke clouds formed in the arena that lingered through the long night. The next seven hours featured musical performances by local favorite Bob Seger, Teegarden and Van Winkle, Phil Ochs, Commander Cody and His Lost Planet Airmen ("Hot Rod Lincoln"), the Up, and jazz saxophonist Archie Shepp. While instruments and amplifiers were rotated between acts, the audience heard revolutionary rhetoric from Rennie Davis, Bobby Seale, Jerry Rubin, and others who had come to Ann Arbor to free an imprisoned pothead; each of the speakers also brought his own take on the Movement's priorities.

Davis gave an impassioned speech that put our government's hypocrisy in perspective: since Sinclair began his sentence two years earlier, American forces—under Nixon's orders—had dropped bombs on Southeast Asia at the rate of "two and a half Hiroshima's a week"—at the same time as the administration tried to convince America that the war was winding down.[17]

Black Panther cofounder Seale let loose a free-verse, poetic rant on the "historical pollution" of war, hunger, murder, injustice—a rhythmic chant that long predated the cadence of rap: "The only solution to pollution is a people's humane revolution!"

Rubin was typically excited, and made sweeping pronouncements on the state of the hippie union. "To all the people who say the Movement, the revolution is over, they ought to see what's going on right here," Rubin observed. "It doesn't look over to me."

Perhaps the most intriguing of Rubin's statements—at least for certain members of the audience—were speculations on what might take place the following year at the 1972 Republican Convention, which at the time was scheduled to be held in California.

"We should do to the Republicans what we did to the Democrats in 1968," Rubin said. "Bring a million to San Diego."

Fellow Chicago Seven veteran Dave Dellinger made similar references, including plans for a political concert. "We want John out of prison," Dellinger said, "to organize the music in San Diego."[18]

It wasn't just the radicals; the concert and Lennon's appearance quickly sparked a bandwagon. Knowing that new laws were set to pass to reduce the penalties for marijuana possession, and equally aware of a Beatle-brightened spotlight on the cause, calls for Sinclair to be released gained momentum. A statement read during the concert from Ann Arbor mayor Robert J. Harris called Sinclair's sentence a "horror" and "disgrace." Harris praised the state legislature for revising pot laws; the East Lansing City

Council agreed with a resolution in support of Sinclair's appeal motion.

"Nothing like this has ever happened in history," Leni Sinclair said, her primary focus on getting back a husband and father. "And it won't be the last time—it's too much fun."

Arrangements were made for Sinclair himself to address the crowd; he snuck his way to a prison pay phone for a quick call to Ann Arbor. Andrews went onstage, stopped the show, and announced: "Ladies and gentlemen, we have a live phone call from Jackson."

"I'm so wiped out I don't know what to say," Sinclair told the audience. He asked the crowd to "say something to me," and the night's loudest cheer went up in an emotional outpouring.

For many, the musical highlight of the night came at one a.m. when a special, unannounced guest star hit the stage. Andrews says he had only learned about the late addition a few days earlier.

"I was sitting in the office and the phone rings," Andrews recalls. "It's Stevie Wonder. After we got John Lennon, nothing's going to surprise me, and Stevie Wonder said he wanted to be part of it."

Wonder—a Motown success beginning at age thirteen whose musical genius shone early and bright—was careful with his politics. Andrews said the singer wanted to make it clear that he neither advocated nor supported the use of drugs, but that "he knew what they did to Sinclair and it wasn't too nice."

Wonder launched into "For Once in My Life." Backstage, Lennon's ears perked up; he hadn't known the Motown star was on the bill. Lennon scrambled to find Andrews and get near the stage.

"Stevie Wonder is here?" Lennon cried in disbelief. "I gotta see him."

Andrews hesitated, picturing John Lennon in the crowd.

"You don't parade a Beatle around the audience," Andrews told the star.

"You have to understand," Lennon explained, "Stevie Wonder is my Beatles."

A squad of security men formed a circle and Lennon was brought through the tunnel to the side of the stage. It wasn't long before people nearby took their eyes off Wonder and gasped in recognition. Crowds formed, too close for Andrews's comfort.

"I told John it was getting messy, and like a trooper he obeyed," Andrews recalls. "He thanked me . . . he was like a kid, seeing Stevie Wonder."

Wonder was uncharacteristically blunt about his politics and music that night. He played Sly Stone's "Somebody's Watching You," which he dedicated to the FBI and "any of the undercover agents who might be out in the audience." Addressing the reason for the concert, Wonder questioned a justice system that jailed Sinclair while the Ohio National Guard faced no charges: "A man gets ten years in prison for possession of marijuana, and another can kill four students at Kent State and walk free. What kind of shit is that? Sometimes I get very disgusted and very discouraged."

Eight hours after the concert started, Lennon took the stage for a short set of four as-yet-unrecorded songs: "Attica State," "The Luck of the Irish," "Sisters O Sisters," and the evening's tribute ballad, "John Sinclair." Lennon was introduced by David Peel, who sang a song in their honor before the introduction.

("John Lennon, Yoko Ono, New York City is your friend," he chanted in his deadpan style.)

Lennon walked on with limited fanfare to enthusiastic applause, wearing a leather jacket and sunglasses and carrying two guitars. Onstage, Lennon introduced "Attica State," which he explained he had started writing "as an ad lib" during his thirty-first birthday celebration in October, but since then "we finished it up." A sound check—"hello, hello" into the microphone—gave way to a thumping start to the song.

The performance wasn't among Lennon's best, a fact obvious to everyone including the singer. Several times during the set Lennon conferred midsong with his back-up players, visibly frustrated. Some of the reviews were critical: "Hardly worth the wait," wrote Bill Gray in the *Detroit News*. Gray wasn't impressed with the "unfamiliar" songs or Yoko's vocal on "Sisters O Sisters."[19]

Lennon prefaced "John Sinclair" with a few remarks. He tuned his steel guitar while he addressed the crowd, speaking to his friends plain and simple as he always did. He was there to help Sinclair, of course, and "spotlight what's going on," but the message he wanted to spread was bigger than just one man in prison.

Lennon's speech was a keynote for a new era. He wanted people to know that passive indifference and benign protest belonged back in the sixties with the Beatles records.

"Apathy isn't it . . . we can do something. So flower power didn't work," Lennon shrugged. "So what, we start again."

Lennon sang: "Free John now, if we can, from the clutches of the man."

About forty-eight hours later they did just that.

CHAPTER 2

JOHN AND
THE ELEPHANTS

*"The music they are planning
to use to crumble the morals of America is the rotten,
filthy, dirty, lewd, lascivious
junk called rock and roll."*

—JACK VAN IMPE

JOHN LENNON HAD said he'd felt somehow restricted on Beatles records, that there were limits on an individual's voice when
performing as part of a group. The intensely personal songs on
his first true solo album in December 1970, *John Lennon / Plastic
Ono Band*, are considered among his finest work. *Plastic Ono Band*
took a stripped down approach long before the term "unplugged"
defined back-to-basics music. For Lennon it was simply an artistic
choice: raw, naked emotion worked better with fewer instruments. Few artists reveal inner pain more openly than Lennon's

performance of "Mother," inspired by the trendy "primal scream" psychotherapy he'd tried; the lyrics that describe his absent father and the loss of Julia Lennon are among his most painfully honest.

Lennon had settled into Manhattan just as his second post-Beatles LP, *Imagine*, was released in September 1971. An enthusiastic Lennon told *New Musical Express* magazine it was "the best thing I've ever done."[1] The band was great, he said, and included "a guy called George Harrison . . . George used to be with the Bubbles or somebody," and he expected the album to satisfy his more commercially minded fans. "This will show them. It's not a personal thing like the last album, but I've learned a lot and this is better in every way. It's lighter, too—I was feeling very happy."

Reviewers were uncertain what to make of it: Good, of course, but not as groundbreaking as *Plastic Ono Band*. The album includes introspective moments such as "Crippled Inside," along with more conventional songwriting like "Jealous Guy" and the playful "Oh Yoko." Lennon's edgier side comes across in a bitter ode to Paul McCartney, "How Do You Sleep," and politics domi-nate the Nixon-baiting "Gimme Some Truth."

Critics acknowledged the rhetoric of revolution, but expected nothing less than genius from Lennon, both musically and ideologi-cally. *Rolling Stone*'s Ben Gerson offered observations about the man as much as the music: "John Lennon has carved out a new career for himself—as political gadfly, floating member of the international avant-garde and rock's most psychologically daring tightrope artist. The other side of the coin is that he hasn't fallen into the latter-day complacency of various other rock and roll over-achievers."[2]

Gerson gave a brief nod to the title track's philosophical offering: "The consolidation of primal awareness into a world movement," and how Lennon asked us to imagine a world without religions or nations, "and that such a world would mean brotherhood and peace." He described Lennon's singing as "methodical but not really skilled, the melody undistinguished except for the bridge, which sounds nice to me."

Mostly the review wondered about the absence of a self-reflecting Lennon, the introspective poet of a generation, now given to social commentary. In "Gimme Some Truth," Lennon said he'd had enough of "schizophrenic-egocentric-paranoiac-prima-donnas." Was the singer unwittingly playing "truthteller" about himself?

"Who is he speaking about now?" Gerson asked. "It seems to me that John is facing the most extraordinary challenge of his career, both personally and artistically. But then, great artists, of whom John is one, are nothing if not resourceful."

"Gimme Some Truth" was Lennon's coming-to-America calling card; he was willing to try new things but tired of lies no matter the source. Invoking a popular Nixonian nickname, Lennon warned: "No short-haired, yellow-bellied son of Tricky Dickie is gonna mother-Hubbard soft-soap me with just a pocketful of hope."

•　　•　　•

WHETHER THE CRITICS were ready for the new role he cast for himself, Lennon welcomed fresh ideas, either from the leaders of America's Left or an almost indiscriminately broad spectrum of artists, both musical and visual, and provocateurs. "They were seeking direction about how to get into what was happening in New York," John Sinclair says. "Never underestimate the role of Yoko Ono in that transformation. She was already a leading figure in the counterculture in America, especially in the arts of the early 1960s."

As eagerly as Lennon was welcomed and sought after by the highest levels of show business and radical politics, the avant-garde art world considered Yoko a leading figure in her own right. Shortly before moving to the Village the Lennons had spent a September weekend in Syracuse, New York, for the opening of "This Is Not Here," the first major American showcase of Yoko's work at the Everson Museum of Art. Museum Director Jim Harithas told the *Syracuse Post-Standard* that conceptual art was well regarded, and Yoko was "one of the earliest and most brilliant exponents."[3]

Conceptual art was misunderstood by mainstream, suburban America, its abstract symbolism dismissed if not ridiculed. A *Syracuse Post-Standard* editorial called the exhibit "an affront to good taste," and not just for the art. Equal disdain was showered on the museum for inviting to town a man who once claimed he was more popular than Christ.

Lennon responded in a letter addressed to "whoever wrote that Hokum about ART."[4] He liked to think he had some knowledge of art, Lennon wrote, and how long artists had suffered the barbs of talentless critics:

> *I'd forgotten about people like you! Well well—you still exist, of course, in other small towns across the*

> *world . . . What on earth has what the husband of*
> *the artist said, four or five years ago, got to do with*
> *the current show at Everson Museum? Artists down*
> *the centuries have been up against bourgeois mealy*
> *mouthed gossip from the "grey people" (or Blue*
> *Meanies!). Society only likes dead artists.*
>
> *P.S. Why don't you come and see the art—I'm sure*
> *the man you think I insulted would turn the other*
> *cheek and come.*

Among the thousands who did attend the show were luminaries including Bob Dylan, Dennis Hopper, and—lured by Yoko rather than Lennon—Andy Warhol, whose Factory included musicians, artists, and filmmakers that were among the Lennons' new downtown neighbors, a colorful cast as comfortable with Yoko's work as they were Lennon's music.

"She was out there, man," Sinclair says. "You'd just see crazy shit where people would come up with scissors and cut her clothes off. Nobody was doing anything like that at all, and she met [Lennon] as a result of her weird art show in London."

Yoko's art pieces included a ladder to climb, atop which a spyglass revealed a card bearing the word *Yes*; another invited people to pay a coin and hammer a nail into a piece of wood. (Lennon was said to have counter-offered that he'd pay an imaginary coin and pound an imaginary nail.) Other works expanded on the concept he and Yoko introduced in 1969 and called "bagism," which they explained at a press conference from inside two large canvas bags:

"total communication" that prevented appearance-based judgments about race, skin color, fashion, or ethnicity.

"If people did interviews for jobs in a bag," Lennon had told David Frost, "they wouldn't get turned away because they were black or green or [had] long hair."[5]

Lennon brought to New York the same willing curiosity he had held for music and art a decade earlier, an approach that embraced everything from existentialism in Germany to Indian meditation. Lennon knew there were like-minded souls in New York with messages to deliver, both artistic and political; and he knew how to market and make accessible creative ideas better than anyone on the planet. Lennon turned his honeymoon into a bedroom press conference for peace; he bought billboards in a dozen cities across the world that read *War is over . . . if you want it.* These initiatives were, Lennon said, a method for sending a simple message:

We're trying to sell peace like people sell soap or soft drinks, [it's] the only way to get people aware that peace is possible. It isn't just inevitable to have violence, not just war but all forms of violence. We're all responsible for Biafra and Hitler and everything, so we're just saying "Sell Peace." Just stick it in the window. Advertise yourself that you're for peace if you believe in it.

There were inevitable critics, and in response Lennon turned the attention back on the media itself, which meant the message would be repeated. He told *New York Times* writer Gloria Emerson that he was just trying to balance war headlines with positive thoughts, whether with billboards or the honeymoon bed as photo op.

"If I'm going to get on the front page I might as well get on the front page with the word 'peace,'" Lennon said.[6]

Emerson questioned whether Lennon had crossed a line, if he risked looking "ridiculous" with stunts like the bed-ins. She admired Lennon's work and considered him a man of talent and intelligence, albeit one acting foolishly.

"There weren't that many that were siding with him," Sinclair recalls. "How many others were taking out billboards in Times Square for peace? Maybe for their new movie, but not for peace."

Peace was the ultimate goal embraced by New Left leaders and organizers, Yippie activists, civil rights champions, and women's liberationists alike—and everyone recognized the potential Lennon's influence had to bring people together. In turn he was equally eager to meet anyone who was making things happen.

"It wasn't like sycophants congregating," Sinclair says. "He was reaching out to people who were doing things and to bring what he had to the table. That was extraordinary. Usually if you wanted somebody to do something you had to get on your knees and beg. He wanted to be part of something."

•　　•　　•

POLITICALLY CHARGED ROCK and roll was a familiar sound throughout the Village and in the hippest New York bars, where local heroes were held in equal if not greater esteem than chart-topping sensations. Lennon heard rave reviews from Jerry

Rubin, David Peel, and others about a down-and-dirty street band, Elephant's Memory.

Headliners at Max's Kansas City, heard on edgy movie soundtracks, the Elephants practiced their craft at Magnagraphics Studio on Bedford Street, just a few blocks away from Lennon's Bank Street pad. Magnagraphics owner Bob Prewitt remembers the Elephants as true counterculture heroes who stood out from the mainstream recordings made at the studio, a roster that included Sha Na Na; Blue Oyster Cult; bawdy diva Bette Midler; commercial work for the Electric Company; and, within a few years, Kiss. The Elephants were musicians' musicians, capable craftsmen who maintained an underground credibility.

"They were the name on the street," Prewitt says. "There was the establishment, then there were street people. They were a 'power to the people' band, right in the thick of it."

Stan Bronstein, a saxophone player and veteran of Tito Puente's orchestra, and drummer Rick Frank had formed the group in 1967, leading a rotating cast that briefly included Carly Simon on vocals. One story among many in Elephant mythology was that Carly left after members of the band threw her boyfriend down a flight of stairs; they were that kind of group, born in strip bars and befriended by motorcycle gangs.[7]

Inexplicably, the Elephants were initially promoted as a bubblegum pop group on independent label Buddah (*sic*) Records. In spite of the label's lighter reputation, the 1969 *Elephant's Memory* LP featured a time-capsule-worthy photo of the band—including lead singer Michal Shapiro, who replaced Carly in the female vocalist spot—covered in groovy body paint instead of clothing.

The album met limited success, although two songs—"Old Man Willow" and "Jungle Gym at the Zoo"—were featured on the soundtrack of *Midnight Cowboy.* (The gritty portrait of New York street life was originally rated X when released yet garnered critical acclaim, including a Best Picture Academy Award. It was also one of the top-grossing films of 1969 and helped launch the careers of actors Dustin Hoffman and John Voight, serving as a wake-up call to Hollywood studios that—along with the cultural shift of rock music—a new day in cinema had dawned.)

Notable tracks, but hardly the formula for hit records. No second album plans were made at Buddah Records, and the group continued with a revolving-door lineup.

"That's all right too, because they weren't so hot back then," wrote Toby Mamis in 1971.[8] Mamis was an underground boy wonder, a teenage editor of an alternative high school newspaper called the *New York Herald-Tribune* who would later work public relations for Apple Records. Mamis had written that the band's early sound was "an obnoxious sort of cross between Blood, Sweat and Tears and Melanie. They bombed out everywhere they played, and in the record racks as well."

For a new decade the band reclaimed its gritty, from-the-streets approach that matched their lifestyle but hadn't yet translated into the music. The Elephants "resurfaced," Mamis reported, and again paid the dues needed to land a record contract; they performed at festivals, high schools, or wherever they could find an audience.

The Elephants returned to Magnagraphics with a new attitude and songs to match. A 1970 album on Metromedia, *Take It to the Streets*, presents tunes pretty much guaranteed to avoid mass-market radio. The lyrics describe starting fires and killing police officers ("pigs"). One notable track, "Tricky Noses," ends with what a reviewer described as "a sudden blast of gunfire."[9] A modest hit from the album, "Mongoose," brought the Elephants a new level of attention and landed them a weeklong gig at Folk City in July 1971.

"Elephant's Memory Mixes Radicalism and a Rough Sound" read a headline from Mike Jahn in the *New York Times*: "Usually the most political statement made by a group consists of 'V' signs and a modest 'power to the people' now and then. A group shouting 'off the pig' can expect to find difficulty in dealing with the music business establishment. Elephant's Memory . . . is one of the latter."[10]

The *Times* cited the group's previous incarnation as providing "a mild form of good-time jazz rock," but the new lineup of Bronstein, Frank, bassist Gary Van Scyoc, keyboardist Adam Ippolito, and guitarist Crow Eisenberg played "an aggressive, rough and loud rock, punctuated by indignant radicalism." Their attitude screamed as loud as the music: "The group is one of the few New York bands with the courage to persist despite lack of great success."

The Folk City engagement raised the band's profile, and *Billboard* magazine took note of the counterculture attitude they brought to the stage: "They perform with irreverence for musical convention and are sometimes oblivious to the audience. But they convey a good musical sense and a hard driving beat . . . a return to rock and roll."[11]

For the cover of *Take It to the Streets*, the first album's flower-power nudity was replaced with a grainy black-and-white image of the band tearing it up at a protest rally. Hardly teenage heartthrobs, their lack of onstage appeal was described by one fan in *Rolling Stone* as "uglier than a Grateful Dead with five Pigpens," referring to the Dead's drummer. Offstage, club owner Mickey Ruskin said the players maintained some time-honored traditions in lieu of current trends: "It's interesting to see a band that's strung out on booze for a change."[12]

Ruskin owned Max's Kansas City, a Park Avenue South music staple where the Elephants were among the core regulars. The band somehow fit the unconventional world of art, culture, politics, and music at Max's. The Velvet Underground dominated the fabled backroom, and the music at Max's reflected diverse tastes and temperaments: the Elephants in all their ugly glory; gender-bending glam rock pioneers David Bowie and the New York Dolls; and more than a few of the Village's most visible political activists.

The Elephants' five-man ensemble gained considerable experience with the additions of newcomers Van Scyoc and Ippolito; although younger by several years they brought respectable talent to the group. Van Scyoc first found success in his native Pittsburgh with the Dynatones, a pop group on the Hanna-Barbera label that landed a 1966 hit, "The Fife Piper," before disbanding. Van Scyoc made the move to New York in 1968, bass guitar in hand for everything from commercial jingles to stage auditions including a near-miss with the hot new musical, *Hair*. The experience was enough to convince Van Scyoc which way his fortunes lay: "The music business was good for me, better than acting."

Van Scyoc next joined Pig Iron, a New York group of jazz-blues roots that included Ippolito on keyboards; the band's self-titled Columbia album in 1970 included a rendition of Screamin' Jay

Hawkins's "I Put a Spell on You." The exposure brought Van Scyoc studio work at Atlantic with top-shelf talent including Neil Sedaka, and after the band dissolved he quickly landed with the Elephants in early 1971. A solid band, Van Scyoc thought, one with established credentials, a band that could go places so long as the lineup of current band members stayed put.

"The two main guys, Stan and Rick, they were the band," Van Scyoc says. "Stan had all the talent and Rick had all the business. They had a couple different lead singers, a raft of guitar players; I remember going through five guitar players that first year."

When a keyboardist was needed to fill the Elephant ranks, Van Scyoc suggested Ippolito, a New Jersey native destined for a life in music thanks to both dad and grandpa being drummers. Ippolito had followed his Pig Iron days with a brief stint in the musical *Soon*, which closed after just three performances at the Ritz Theater on Forty-Eighth Street. (Notably, the cast featured the debuts of Richard Gere and Nell Carter, and included Barry Bostwick.) "[It was] a rock opera about a band and their managers and groupies," Ippolito says. "I was in the pit band. After that, I was looking around and Gary invited me to play with Elephant's Memory."

Fans may pay allegiance to one genre of music or another, but musicians—those looking to make a dollar with their talent—are open to and understand a range of styles, tastes, and backgrounds. Ippolito was originally schooled in jazz, his passion when he graduated from high school in 1964, the year of "Beatlemania."

"I didn't really think much of the Beatles, to tell the truth," Ippolito says. "In my sophomore year of college a good friend of mine was a voice major and turned me on to the Beatles, the

Beach Boys. By the time I got into that, I wanted to be in music."

With Elephant's Memory, music wasn't necessarily the only factor in an audition. "Rick was probably the political driving force, although Stan happily went along," Ippolito says. "The first night I went down to play with them they asked me what I thought of their politics."

Whether they believed the band could represent the Movement, both Van Scyoc and Ippolito said the group's chances for commercial success improved with the addition of their newest, youngest member, Texas-born guitar player Wayne "Tex" Gabriel.

Gabriel and his mother, Marian, left the Lone Star State while he was an infant in the early 1950s to escape an abusive, largely absent father. Gabriel spent his youth in Detroit's Highland Park, where high school ambitions on the football field were sidelined by an injury. While recuperating, Gabriel took to the guitar with dedicated, natural ease.

Gabriel's first nontelevised look at Lennon was at the Beatles' 1966 Olympia Stadium concert. At the live show, however—as the Beatles themselves realized by then—Gabriel says the music was difficult to judge: "You couldn't hear anything because of the screaming girls. I mean, they were . . . screaming!"

Gabriel did some paid work in Michigan before testing the New York waters in 1970, a trip recalled mostly for a classic car-broke-down-just-west-of-the-Lincoln-Tunnel story. He went home and worked for a few months with Mitch Ryder's Detroit, a revamped Detroit Wheels fronted by the "Devil with a Blue Dress On" singer. The New York dream remained, though, and in the summer of 1971 Gabriel returned to Manhattan for another shot. His mother had died a few months earlier, and was unable to share the good news when Gabriel auditioned for and landed a gig with Elephant's Memory. A promising opportunity, but still very much a struggling-musician existence.

"Tex first moved into Stan's apartment, but it was like a homeless shelter for animals there, dogs and cats and whatnot," Ippolito says. "Wayne had two dogs, so he came to live in my apartment. Wayne slept in the living room, sometimes in the kitchen, but I'm not sure why."

Musically, Van Scyoc said that Gabriel was the answer to the band's prayers.

"When Tex came in from Detroit I said, 'We gotta get this guy,'" Van Scyoc recalls. "He loved the band, we loved him. He was such a phenomenal player, I remember telling my wife we found a new Eric Clapton."

Among his first gigs with the band was their return engagement at Folk City. The impression he made on the group was echoed by the press.

"Wayne Gabriel has only been with Elephant's Memory for a couple of weeks," reported *Variety* on December 8. "He fits in well, even having his own tune, 'Life' included in the set. Elephant's Memory's reputation is starting to grow."

The brighter spotlight, Van Scyoc points out, was a dubious benefit. The music-for-the-masses crusade had become a strain and he was considering other options as 1971 drew to a close.

"I was really tired of doing no-money gigs," Van Scyoc admits.

•   •   •

> *What a waste of human power,*
> *What a waste of human lives*
> *Shoot the prisoners in the towers*
> *Forty-three poor widowed wives.*
> —JOHN LENNON, "Attica State"

ON DECEMBER 16, only a week after he played before thousands of concertgoers who partied and rallied on behalf of a jailed poet in Michigan, Lennon filmed an episode of old friend David Frost's talk show, now broadcast from New York. Lennon and Yoko took their seats at the edge of a circular riser in an intimate theater, the audience before them just feet away.[13]

Small talk gave way quickly to "Attica State." Lennon played acoustic guitar, accompanied by Yoko and Rubin on bongos and two guitarists from the Lower East Side band.

The topic was fresh in the minds of New Yorkers. Just three months earlier, the headlines had been dominated by a riot at Attica, an upstate prison. In a response to the shooting death of California inmate George Jackson, more than 1,200 New York prisoners had seized control of Attica to demand prison reform. Governor Nelson Rockefeller sent along upward of 1,700 troops to take control by any means necessary, and the ensuing battle ended in a controversial bloodbath.

Singing about Attica before Frost's studio audience, Lennon went further with his lyrics than he had in previous songs and peace anthems. "Attica State" was blunt and specific as it reported the body count from the victims' perspective: "Forty-three poor widowed wives." Lennon sang that the "media blames it on the prisoners," but word on the street held that "Rockefeller pulled the trigger."

The song ended with Lennon repeating the chorus lyric: "We're all mates with Attica State." Polite applause followed.

For many New Yorkers, the suggestion that "all they need is love and care" was not a practical solution, not in a city with crime rates that ranked among the highest in the world. It was a tense time on both sides of the law: Frank Serpico—a longhair hippie cop who lived in the Village—told the internal investigation Knapp Commission in May 1971 of the near-epidemic graft and kickbacks in the NYPD. Serpico's one-man crusade had ended earlier that year when he was shot during a February drug raid, an ambush likely choreographed by fellow officers.

John Lennon challenged the Manhattan audience. Many were unabashed Beatles fans and in full agreement with one of their generation's leading spokesmen. They loved John, and might agree with him about civil rights, women's liberation, gay rights and ending the Vietnam War—but didn't quite see eye-to-eye with him about Attica.

Some voiced their opinions from the balcony and main floor. Lennon and Frost peered up, tried to see who was speaking through the glare of stage lights, and wanted to make sure they understood the question.

"We can't hear you up there," Lennon said. "Why don't you come down here?"

Frost stood, repeated the invitation, and made room near the stage. A woman and a man, both in their midthirties, took seats in the front row, eye-level with Lennon.

The fourth wall between audience and entertainer came down. Few artists had ever stood as elevated by their audience as the Beatles; fewer still could sit with the same fans in casual comfort. They might as well have been in a living room with friends watching and discussing the evening news.

Of course Attica was a tragedy, the woman said, but Lennon's song "made it sound like the only worthwhile people in this world are people who committed crimes."

The "forty-three poor widowed wives," Lennon replied, included everyone affected by the deaths. "We're talking about policemen's wives, anyone who was hurt there." The word "prisoners" was used in broad terms: "Free the prisoners, free the judges, free all prisoners everywhere."

New Yorkers, the woman said, couldn't afford such an approach. "I'm in prison, living in New York," she added, describing a life spent clutching her purse and "being afraid to walk into my home." These problems were not as simple as Lennon made them out to be; they weren't curable by people saying "peace and love."

"You'll solve it by bringing up children differently," she said, "or by having a better penal system. But not by making heroes out of people who hold knives to people's throats."

Lennon admitted that there was no easy solution.

"I understand that society hasn't worked out what to do with people who kill, and violent people," Lennon said. "We're not glorifying them. This song will come and go, but there will be another Attica tomorrow."

The topic—Attica—was specific, Lennon said, and was one of several contemporary issues that he wrote about as a form of musical journalism, the traveling minstrel weaving melodic folktales.

"We're like newspapermen, only we sing about it," Lennon observed.

There were few things New Yorkers loved more than weighing in on the day's headlines. Angry letters to the editor read the same whether in print or addressed to an ex-Beatle on a talk show.

"Wait till they kill your son or daughter or your mother or father," the man shouted. "You talk about what society's done to them. Walk through one of those neighborhoods at two in the morning. You wouldn't be singing about the people who ended up in jail for mugging you."

Frost moderated the back-and-forth objectively, gave equal time to opposing views, and raised a variety of related topics along the way. Lennon, Frost said, brought intelligence and passion to his new work, as he always had.

"This is an example of the fact that John is writing songs, passing on what he cares about," Frost remarked.

Lennon seemed frustrated, if undaunted, and was eager to get back on more comfortable ground.

"Let's sing another song," Lennon said. He sang of John Sinclair, and of the troubles in Northern Ireland with "Luck of the Irish." He'd come to America to do just that, to find places and reasons to sing. He told the Frost audience about his next gig, a benefit to support the families of Attica victims at Harlem's landmark Apollo Theater.

"We've been invited to play the song and just go there to show that we care," Lennon said. "We'll go along and sing it if they want us to or just say hello, just to show people that we don't live in an ivory tower in Hollywood watching movies about ourselves, and that we care about what's going on."

The night after recording the Frost show, Lennon appeared as promised at the Apollo, where he basked in the spotlight along with some of the musicians that had most inspired him. John and Yoko—again backed by Rubin and Lower East Side guitarists Chris Osbourne and Eddie Mottau—were a last-minute addition to the program and seemed to surprise the audience. Gasps were heard when an announcer stood before the curtain "to introduce a young man and his wife who saw fit to put down in music and lyrics so that it will never be forgotten . . . the tragedy of Attica State."

Lennon said it was "an honor and a pleasure" to be at the Apollo, and counted down the beat before launching into "Attica State." The audience didn't question the lyrics or position, and signaled their agreement that "Rockefeller pulled the trigger" with spirited shouts and applause. Lennon played just three songs—"Attica State," "Sisters O Sisters," and "Imagine," which he introduced as "a song you might know" while he strummed the opening chords on his guitar.

The Apollo show marked the third public performance by Lennon in barely a week's time, appearances that were kept brief and in which John appeared almost apologetic. Lennon again explained the shortcomings to the audience.[14]

"Some of you wonder what I'm doing here with no drummers and nothing like that," Lennon said. "Well, you might know I lost my old band, or I left it." He'd been trying to put a band together, he said, but he'd been busier than expected in recent weeks.

Lennon never cared if some people misunderstood his art or politics, but subpar music was unacceptable no matter how amusing he found David Peel. After the Apollo show Lennon made it a top priority to identify the right group of musicians for the ambitious plans now underway. Lennon's new friend Jerry Rubin said he had just the band in mind, straight from the heart of Greenwich Village.

•   •   •

BOB PREWITT SAYS he was warned ahead of time to keep John Lennon's meeting with Elephant's Memory a low-profile affair. The warning probably wasn't necessary. The Elephant's Memory band members were as serious about the music as John was.

As a musician Lennon was equal parts avid fan and perfectionist artist. He enjoyed, encouraged, and celebrated creative people, even the often-amateur quality of Village dreamers and dabblers, but held his own performances to elite Beatles' standards. He'd soldiered through the Ann Arbor, David Frost, and Apollo sets with Peel's Lower East Side band and the percussion talents of Yoko and Jerry Rubin, but there were bigger plans in the works: television appearances, studio recordings, and taking the show on the road. The man needed a band.

Rubin had played a recording of Elephant's Memory for Lennon—a performance broadcast on Long Island's WLIL-FM (a show that also featured a young piano player from Oyster Bay named Billy Joel). The sounds of Stan Bronstein's blistering saxophone and Wayne Gabriel's sharp-edged guitar work impressed Lennon, who agreed to a meeting at Magnagraphics.

The members of Elephant's Memory had no idea what to expect, and quickly learned that Lennon was not as easy to define as many assumed. On their first meeting, Lennon did what he often did—he used humor to break the ice, to deflect the standard "Oh my God, it's a Beatle" reaction. Lennon turned it around and expressed amazement at meeting the Elephants.

"Are you them?" Lennon asked, saying he'd heard so much about the group. "Are you *really* them?" Playing it for laughs was an approach he mastered whether the room was filled with hippies or heads of state, rockers or royalty.

"Yeah," chuckled drummer Rick Frank. "Are you really him?"

The band kept it cool, being the sophisticated, hip players they were. While they weren't complete strangers to the world of A-list musicians, Prewitt recalls that "seeing him in the flesh for the first time was kind of a shock. All these thoughts start running through your head: *Jesus, that's actually John Lennon!* I didn't want to stare, but the gravity of it struck me—the possibilities were endless."

No freak show, but a certain circus atmosphere filled the air: Lennon wore what appeared to be the white suit from *Abbey Road*; the beard was gone, his hair was cropped shorter than the Jesus-twin of the Beatles' swan song; but the image he presented still invoked memories of the surreal sixties.

Light banter gave way to common ground—music—and that's where the deal was clinched. They played for hours, running through dozens of rock and roll classics: "Hound Dog," "Dizzy Miss Lizzy," some Chuck Berry tunes. By evening's end the Elephants had the gig of a lifetime.

"Both John and Yoko were very impressed," Gabriel recalls.

"He said we sounded great, and that he really liked us a lot. Of course, we already kind of loved him."

Prewitt's control-room vantage point took in the scene, an admittedly rough-around-the-edges band playing with a legend. Drummer Rick Frank, who once called himself "Reek Havoc" and pounded through life in the Keith Moon–worthy tradition of lunatic percussionists, scaled down his savage act in front of Lennon. "He was a wild man," Prewitt says of Frank. "To see him subdued and respectful, like a little kid, it was interesting."

A contract was offered: Elephant's Memory was put on retainer and began rehearsals to learn a concert's worth of Lennon songs. There were meetings with Apple Records to schedule a Lennon-produced Elephant's Memory album along with the *Some Time in New York City* sessions. Lennon's 1972 calendar—with or without the Yippies—promised to be busy.

"He mentioned a TV show coming up," Gabriel says. "And that he wanted us to meet Phil Spector, who would produce an album we were going to do."

Plucked from comparative obscurity, this one-in-a-million shot brought as much pressure as promise; playing with Lennon was a chance for the Elephants to prove their musical worth.

"They were proud of being a good band," Prewitt says. "They had a great sound and were very competent musicians."

Emotions were mixed: excitement over meeting a Beatle, disbelief over the prospect of working with one. In show business terms it was very much a double-edged opportunity.

"Our careers were basically on the line," says Van Scyoc.

•   •   •

JOHN SINCLAIR KNEW what his priorities were when he walked out of prison in early December 1971. He cheerfully told reporters that, first, "I'm gonna go home and smoke some joints, man."

The second thing was to pay a thank-you visit to the man he considered responsible for his release.

"Because John Lennon came, it sold," Sinclair says. "They made the connection that, Jesus, 'If a Beatle thinks this guy is all right, we should let him out.' That's the mass mind turning when John Lennon said he was coming."

The court approved Sinclair's bond for a number of reasons—including the state legislature reducing pot possession from a felony to a misdemeanor—but it was Lennon who made it happen as quickly as it did. Sinclair wasn't alone in believing his release represented more than one man's freedom: "Here's this guy in prison for marijuana and we got him out three days later. That's the mythology to build on," he says.

Celebrity endorsements were nothing new—famous faces have a long history of plugging everything from breakfast cereal and cigarettes to candidates—but the politically minded hippies and Yippies knew that Lennon's influence was something much bigger. Might the Jesus-effect that had forced open the prison gates for Sinclair tilt the scales against Nixon in the upcoming 1972 presidential election?

"It was a great example," Sinclair says. "See what would happen if the people whose records you liked would also support the other people you like. This could create a thing across the country that people could rally around."

In the final week of 1971 John and Leni Sinclair flew to New York and brought a celebratory atmosphere to an increasingly popular and crowded Bank Street apartment. Jerry Rubin had been spreading the word of the Lennon-Yippie alliance in the media, and had promised to take John and Yoko "to the center of the revolution." Bank Street became that hub. Guests that month included the famous and not so famous, the celebrated and notorious. For every musical guest—Lower East Side players or wandering Elephants—there was an activist, including Rubin, Rennie Davis, Stew Albert, Black Panther founders Huey Newton and Bobby Seale, feminist Kate Millet, poet Ed Sanders, and countless others.

This was the Movement. These were radical leaders fighting to shake up the system and take down the establishment, the same ones as put fear in the hearts of conservative Americans who worried that the longhair freaks represented a Communist threat . . . or worse. During one gathering Rubin played a tape he thought Lennon would enjoy, a fire-and-brimstone sermon by evangelist Jack Van Impe on the evils he found in Rubin's book, *Do It*. Rubin's pages not only contained "178 four-letter words," it foretold a perverted revolution, pure Sodom and Gomorrah in America: "Sex in the streets of every major city from coast to coast!"[15]

Van Impe's outrage put the blame where he thought it should be for the proposed national orgy, a sexual frenzy driven by sinful songs: "The music they are planning to use to crumble the morals of America is the rotten, filthy, dirty, lewd, lascivious junk called rock and roll." Van Impe remained unconvinced by young congregants who claimed that many rock songs held spiritual offerings of peace and love. A false front, he said. "God help compromising preachers who allow this rock beat into pulpits just because it has 'Jesus Saves' tied to it," Van Impe said. "It isn't just the words, it's the beat."

Lennon laughed. He'd heard the cries of rock and roll as the devil's music for as long as he'd played electric guitar. Ironically, people like Van Impe actually underestimated rock's potential power, at least as wielded by a Beatle. There were bigger ideas being kicked around Bank Street than Rubin's antic predictions of sex in the streets: Could the same type of concert that freed a man from prison be taken on the road as a political tour?

The Sinclair concert was the prototype, the test-run for a national caravan in tandem with the 1972 political campaigns. A roaming cast of activists, poets, and artists gathered with local players and politicians to raise money for local causes, encourage voter registration, and frame a political agenda for the eighteen-to-twenty-year-old rookie voters ready to make important electoral choices. Bank Street speculations were confirmed when the principal planners met in late December at the Peter Stuyvesant farm in Allamuchy, New Jersey. At the Allamuchy meeting Rennie Davis made a concrete offer to Lennon.

"I proposed to John that we go to forty-two cities that had been selected strategically; each city was going to have one focus or issue," Davis says, a momentum that would build and peak at the Republican convention. "I was very positive about what this could mean, but I didn't really know for sure if we could pull it off. We were declining, and John coming in was pulling us out of this swamp. I was curious about how this was going to work."

Any disbelief or apprehensions gave way to enthusiasm when the idea received John's official blessing. Jay Craven, a Boston University activist who had been serving as Davis's right-hand man since the two met when Davis visited the campus, represented the next generation of activists. Although only a few years behind Rubin, Davis, and Hoffman, Craven and his contemporaries considered themselves more practical-minded than their predecessors.

"We weren't the flower children, who were the children of the Beatles in some ways," Craven says. The big battles of the civil rights movement had already been fought, and he preferred local activism. "That generation of Rennie and the Chicago Seven never really opened the door to my generation. We weren't in SDS, we didn't have the same noble-esque views of organization."

A national tour starring John Lennon would take more than a little organizing to pull off; ready or not, the plan became real at the New Jersey meeting.

"I was taken aside by Rennie and Jerry Rubin," Craven recalls. "They said John Lennon and Yoko Ono want to work with us, and they're prepared to go on the road and do whatever in a bus with a boogie band."

Lennon would headline and attract the musicians; Davis was to line up speakers and causes. Each show would feature an unannounced surprise guest, as Ann Arbor did with Stevie Wonder, building to an August finale pairing Lennon with Bob Dylan.

The idea seemed every bit as "brilliant" as Sinclair imagined, but Davis had seen inflated expectations fall victim to apathy or disorganization. He wanted to make sure that there would be the sustained effort and dedicatin required to make the tour a success.

The logistics of the tour would be handled by Davis and Craven, who understood the mechanics of organizing something as massive as a twenty-city political-musical tour. There were increasing doubts about the effectiveness of Abbie Hoffman and Jerry Rubin, who both were more into their own writing projects by this time and probably distracted more than a little by their own celebrity. Hoffman debuted as an author in 1971 with *Steal This Book*, which promoted a life of not spending money, and was working on the 1972 effort *Vote*, coauthored with Rubin and Ed Sanders.

"Jerry and Abbie were writing their books, doing their thing, occasionally invoking the Yippie creed in action or comment," Craven says. They were highly quotable media darlings, but had little involvement in the nuts-and-bolts of planning effective demonstrations. Davis was a strong organizer, but had been fighting the fight for a long time by then.

"Rennie was pretty burned out, exhausted," Craven notes. "He felt that the Movement had just peaked and essentially deflated."

As 1972 began, Craven was set to be the advance man. The strategy was to have the caravan follow the election cycle beginning in states with the earliest primaries and largest populations. The tour would support a number of causes, but according to Craven there was to remain a singular focus: "Making the war the central issue of the 1972 election. Any candidate who did not clearly oppose the war would be isolated and go down in defeat. Nixon [had] continued the war and had to pay the price for it."

On paper, the idea was an ambitious yet achievable plan. Lennon told *Rolling Stone* it was all set for '72.[16] Politics aside, Lennon was eager to play benefit concerts that would promote local causes such as day care centers, food co-ops, and health clinics. The real perk for John, however, remained that this would mark his return to the musical spotlight:

> *I just want to be a musician and transmit some love back to the people. That's what excited me the most, getting to play with a band again. It will be the regular scene without the capitalism. We'll pay for the halls and the people will have to pay to get in but we'll leave our share of the money in town where it can do the most good. We want it to be the regular scene except we also want to raise some consciousness.*

Some of Lennon's ambitions—to be just another New Yorker, just another guy on the street, or to be just another player in the band and not its shining star—bordered on naïveté, but in a spirit he carried off with playful innocence as he fell in love with Manhattan and his new band. He hinted that his work with Elephant's Memory would be long-range and artistically inclusive. He told the *Village Voice* the relationship would more closely resemble "Dylan and the Band rather than McCartney's Wings," both an idealistic statement and an open shot at his former bandmate's new project.[17]

And so the free-for-all circus on Bank Street and in New Jersey welcomed all comers to the cause. Planning meetings included a young woman who took the minutes with a steno book but was not, Leni Sinclair recalls, part of the Movement; she instead turned out to be an informant. The FBI had for some time kept their eyes and ears on Rubin, Davis, and their associates. Heading into 1972, they added former Beatle John Lennon to the list.

•   •   •

LENNON MAY HAVE been uncertain about—and soon started to demonstrate caution toward—his new political friends, but as always he took solace in the music. Forming new relationships with musicians perhaps made the thirty-one-year-old nostalgic for the salad days when the Beatles were still a yet-unrealized dream.

Lennon enjoyed simply jamming with his new band; playing music in the studio, at clubs, even on the occasional street corner—which they did one evening—made him feel at home and were all equally suitable venues. It was a simple pleasure that had been lost to Lennon once the screaming girls drowned out the melodies at Beatles' concerts. And the music itself was more than just the music: they hung out together, jammed for a while, got to know one another. "The inner workings of a band," Van Scyoc calls it. "Like being married to four other guys."

Lennon tried to ignore the pressure he and those connected with him must have felt in writing a sequel to the Beatles. Although it was obvious to everyone in the room that the

Elephants were auditioning to be supporting players, Lennon tried to put them at ease with tongue-in-cheek goofiness.

"John asked if he could join our band," Van Scyoc says. "We looked at each other saying: 'What the hell? That's not going to work! What do we call it? What's the media going to say?'"

As if Lennon gave a damn about the press reaction to his decisions—a man who held a press conference while wrapped in a bag with his wife. At the same time, there were things about which Lennon cared very much, primarily the music. Most everything else was a lark: the Beatles admitted that their forays into movies were largely done for a laugh, their concerts had become a noisy joke, and press conferences were an excuse for British silliness in the Goons–Monty Python tradition. Yet few bands ever treated recording sessions with such dedication, nor acted stronger as a team with a shared respect for the final product.

Could that happen again in New York? Lennon approached his new life in Manhattan with the same cheerful gusto so many experience when moving there. Lennon marveled at the change in atmosphere between Greenwich Village and Times Square, from Wall Street's concrete canyons to Central Park. He described the neighborhood seen from behind his circular glasses to Hendrik Hertzberg of the *New Yorker*: "It's like a quaint little town . . . like a little Welsh village, with Jones the Fish and Jones the Milk and everybody seems to know everybody." He pedaled a bicycle through narrow downtown streets, dropped in without fanfare at the outrageous Village shops and happening places. Tex Gabriel recalls casual times with Lennon, just wandering Manhattan, maybe stopping for breakfast at the Pink

Teacup restaurant on Grove Street.

"He wanted to be out walking the streets, which we did many times," says Gabriel. "For the most part nobody bothered him. Of course, people did come up to ask for an autograph, and he would graciously abide." There were times when the attention was too much, too strong, and Lennon would politely say "that's all," and walk—not run—away, but Lennon was generally friendly and appreciative when encountered by fans.

Lennon felt free in the big city, anonymous among the crowds. The relative newcomer played eager tour guide when John and Leni Sinclair visited and took them to a restaurant on Ninety-First Street called, simply, Home. To Lennon it was a life that would have seemed impossible in London, but he'd convinced himself—for whatever reasons—that he could enjoy life's simple pleasures in America.

"It's a big deal when you go out in public and don't have any life of your own, you're just this fantasy of people who bought your record," John Sinclair says. "Lennon wanted to be an artist. He didn't want to be the head of the fucking Beatles anymore with the girls screaming; he did that."

It was a far cry from his final days in England, where the privacy of his home was shattered by fans who wanted more than just musical memories, where the press sharpened their pens to attack his wife, where every street held Beatles memories he wanted to put in the past.

"In London they couldn't do that, they had people camped outside their house," Sinclair says. "Jesus Christ, what a punishment for making good records."

CHAPTER 3

"DOPED WITH RELIGION AND SEX AND TV"

"We'd like to talk about love, peace, communicating, women's liberation, racism, war. That's what's going on."
—JOHN LENNON on the *Mike Douglas Show*

JOHN LENNON WASN'T being paranoid; he was being watched, even more than in the usual music-fan fishbowl way that had been his life for years by now.

He was a celebrity, of course, and even on the jaded New York streets he attracted attention. The Bank Street residence was fairly well known in the neighborhood, his rehearsals with Elephant's Memory at Magnagraphics common knowledge. Much of it was familiar, whether in London or America: people lingered near his home or recording studio who wanted nothing more than the gentle smile and quick autograph he offered without pause.

But something more was going on. The same men—who didn't look like they belonged in the West Village—seemed rooted to nearby parking spaces; Lennon's studio-trained ears picked up on more than just static on the telephone line. Photographer Bob Gruen, a neighbor familiar with the quiet street, had become a friend of John and Yoko's and remained so throughout the decade. In a photo book published years later Gruen recalled when the local climate changed: "My neighbors told me they often spotted guys out on Bank Street wearing trench coats and the trademark fedoras. These men would ask passersby if they'd noticed anything suspicious about John and Yoko."[1]

"What became clear was that the surveillance on John and Yoko was intensifying," says Jay Craven, whose activities were likewise monitored. "There was a sense of danger," he continues. "There was a desire by the government to make them feel that their every move and every word was being monitored. That clearly made John nervous."

Craven was well acquainted with life under surveillence; he'd spent enough time in the company of what the Federal Bureau of Investigation called "known radicals," including Rennie Davis, Jerry Rubin, and others in the Movement, documents that included references to his involvement.

"The FBI knew everything that was going on," Craven says.

Lennon's name began appearing in federal reports as plans for the concert tour were laid at the start of an election year, linking him with those considered a threat to national security.

A New York bureau agent reported on January 4, 1972, that Rubin and activist Stewart Albert were "in constant contact with John Lennon in New York. Reasons unknown (possibly financial)." A January 6 follow-up hinted that the first concert might take place that March in New Hampshire, and would include "John Lennon, of the Beatles."[2]

Craven spent much of January setting the foundation for the planned tour, to be run from an office on Hudson Street in a building John and Yoko purchased. He made several snowy trips up and down the eastern seaboard and hauled files and typewriters from the Washington office that he and Rennie Davis had used during previous protests.

This, too, was known in Washington; a January 10 memo reported the relocation and confirmed that the principal players were together in New York. A concert was being planned, but New York field agents didn't call it that. Instead they used terms such as "peace rally" in their reports, and the political nature of the scheme caught the highest attentions possible in Washington: FBI director J. Edgar Hoover was sent a January 23 "priority report" on "protest activities and civil disturbances"; copies went to the very top of the national ladder, including the president, vice president, secretary of state, CIA, and armed services brass.

Hoover's summary first identified those involved, the so-called Allamuchy Tribe, named for the location of the New Jersey meeting that confirmed Lennon's commitment to the tour. Among the leaders of the tribe were "Rennie Davis, one of the defendants in the Chicago Seven trials, and will include Stu Alpert and J. Craven," along with John Lennon.

The "tribe" name coined by the FBI to describe the group was an agent's invention—it wasn't a title that Davis and Craven said was used by those involved—but the reported purpose was clear: "To direct Movement activities during the election year, which activities will culminate with demonstrations at the Republican National Convention."

How those plans would be funded was also cause for concern. A follow-up memo from the New York FBI office for the first time referenced an alleged $75,000 contribution given by Lennon for the tribe's formation, an amount cited in subsequent reports as being the seed money for the Election Year Strategy Information Center—for practical purposes the same group under another name.

Intelligence reports were often precise in their accuracy; other times the investigation seemed amateurish when trying to gather basic facts about a high-profile subject. A February 2 memo reported that John and Yoko vacated their last known residence, the St. Regis hotel: "Lennon has since moved to unknown address." By then, Lennon was several months into his stay at 105 Bank Street; the agent was unable to learn what pretty much everyone in the West Village knew. Perhaps to make sure of identities, the same memo requested background information, "including photo of subject." For some reason, obtaining a photograph in New York City of John Lennon required assistance from HQ.

He wasn't difficult to find. Lennon joined an early February protest—raised-fist photos of John and Yoko were widely published—at the New York office of British Overseas Airways. The demonstration called for the withdrawal of British troops from Northern Ireland in the wake of the Bloody Sunday riots. The agent noted that there was no evidence that Lennon supported the Irish Republican Army militant group and its any-means-necessary stance in their quest for independence from Britain.

Still, Lennon's associations with political activists—under any name—stirred considerable interest: the combination of the radical leaders' history and Lennon's wealth and influence could very well be a political force in the forthcoming election. A bureau summary described Lennon's recent activities, along with the reports by undercover agents at the Ann Arbor concert. John Sinclair's near-immediate release from prison was duly noted. In New York Lennon kept company with Rubin, Davis, Craven, and assorted "New Left leaders," known advocates of a "program to 'dump Nixon'" through a series of rock concerts; people who had been "instrumental in disrupting the 1968 Democratic National Convention in Chicago."

Plans that involved the Chicago Seven—who'd been found guilty of riot-inciting—qualified as a matter of national security. As such, copies were sent to ranking defense officials including the chairman of the Senate Armed Services Committee, long-time South Carolina lawmaker Strom Thurmond.

"This appears to be an important matter," Thurmond wrote in a February 4 cover letter sent with the report to William Timmons, legislative affairs assistant to President Richard Nixon; another copy went to Attorney General John Mitchell. These youth rallies against Nixon might work—certainly with the rookie eighteen-to-twenty-year-old voters—now that they had "John Lennon as a drawing card." The Chicago Seven seemed able to make use of Lennon's name for a show guaranteed to "pour tremendous amounts of money into the coffers of the New Left."

Thurmond advised that the information be strongly considered "at the highest level," and that something should be done about it. "As I can see, many headaches might be avoided if appropriate action be taken in time."

For "appropriate action," Thurmond suggested the obvious solution to a trouble-making foreigner, although it should be done carefully: "If Lennon's visa is terminated it would be a strategy counter-measure. The source also noted the caution which must be taken with regard to the possible alienation of the so-called 18-year-old vote if Lennon is expelled from the country."

The goal for which Lennon's deportation would be good "strategy" was not specified, but referencing eighteen-year-old voters—a real wild card in the upcoming election rather than merely a demographic—strongly suggests that the motivation was the election, not security.

The FBI investigation of John Lennon stands apart, rare if not unique for several reasons: the plan to monitor and deport Lennon came from within the government; the allegation was of what he might do, not anything he'd already done; and the threat was not of potential attacks on America. It was all about the job security of the president. The hippies and Yippies believed that Lennon could influence the election, and so did the politicians holding elected office.

In a report entitled "New 'New Left' Group Formed" in the

February 11 *FBI Current Intelligence Analysis,* Lennon was described as more than just a concert participant casually helping the Election Year Strategy Information Center and its opposition to Nixon, but perhaps its driving force: "Lennon's money and name have placed him in a position of considerable influence in EYSIC. No key planning sessions are held without Lennon."

An image of John Lennon dominated the cover, an illustration rather than a photograph. Apparently, the FBI still couldn't seem to find a picture of one of the world's most photographed men.

•   •   •

"I've been practicing with Elephant's Memory. Have you heard of them? They're a New York band, good musicians. I really like them. They understand everything that's going on, too. I'm going to play with them on the Mike Douglas show."
—JOHN LENNON in *Rolling Stone*[3]

ELEPHANT'S MEMORY WAS well known in New York; people on the downtown scene were accustomed to seeing the band's name in the *Village Voice* or rocking the crowds at Max's Kansas City. Even the youngest man, Tex Gabriel, had already experienced a measure of celebrity in Detroit, onstage with Mitch Ryder before loyal, local fans. But playing with John Lennon was something else entirely.

"It was happening, but it was so bizarre, like I was in some fog, a dream," Gabriel says. "Being that way kept me from going, 'Oh my God, this is John Lennon: I'm going to fuck up so bad!' Your consciousness sometimes protects you from drama; it put me in a surreal mode where I just went along for the ride. Where could it go from there?"

Lennon's musical future was as much a matter of speculation as his political plans. The Elephants were in the unfortunate position of appearing as temporary substitutes in the eyes of fans who would have preferred to see a reunion.

"A lot of people asked him when the Beatles were getting back together," Gabriel says. "He'd just point to us and say, 'These are the Beatles, now.'"

Not quite. The "Plastic Ono Elephant's Memory Band" was not destined to replace the Fab Four by any means; nobody—including a star-studded group featuring Eric Clapton that had played with Lennon in Toronto—would be capable of doing that for any Beatle. Clearly, though, the bandsmen could bask in the reflected spotlight. Bob Dylan's supporting players, simply known as the Band, used their time behind a star of near-Beatle brightness as a launching pad for a sound and style decidedly their own. Could the same thing happen for the veteran Village players?

"I was really rooting for them," Magnagraphics owner Bob Prewitt recalls of the opportunity. "I thought, 'Damn, these guys are really gonna make it.' And . . . yeah . . . if they made it, I was gonna make it with them. Lennon held the promise of putting us all on the map, so to speak. This was perfect."

The band was cautious, however, of the pitfalls of backing a legend. Stan Bronstein and Rick Frank wanted to make sure the Elephants weren't lost in the glare, and Lennon encouraged the group to maintain its identity.

"He wasn't asking them to mimic what he did," Prewitt says. "He wanted the Elephants to maintain autonomy throughout the tracks. He wanted them to be them."

The proximity and hours spent together invited a camaraderie where Lennon was most comfortable—the recording studio. A particular kinship formed between Lennon, whose mother, Julia, was killed by a drunk driver shortly before her son made his first record, and Gabriel, still adjusting to his mother's recent passing.

"They had something of a bond," Van Scyoc says. "Besides the obvious that they were both guitar players, they had a lot in common: Tex's mother just died, and John had lost his mother. It was pretty intense. They were always just sitting there on the floor cross-legged, face-to-face for hours playing and talking."

Getting to know Lennon revealed more than a few surprises to the band. Certainly they held preconceived notions—as had a generation—which they soon learned were often false, usually blurred. To those who didn't really know the man, Lennon was often a complicated puzzle to be solved, a walking contradiction. Was he funny or sarcastic, kind or harsh, generous or self-serving?

Was Lennon arrogant? That was one perception, a smart-ass image dating back to the Beatles' introduction to America on Ed Sullivan's stage, Lennon grinning like he knew something everyone else didn't. Instead the musicians met a man not quite as cocky as they assumed. Lennon was sincerely apologetic, even humble, during his early appearances with improvised bands. Heading into another album, TV appearances, and possible tour, Lennon knew the music would be judged according to an almost impossibly high standard.

"Sometimes I thought he was more nervous than we were," Gabriel says. "It was the first time he'd been with a group other than the Beatles, his buddies, and now he was coming together with this street band."

Then there was Lennon's relationship with Yoko Ono. Some, including the Beatles, had questioned his habit of letting her share stage time or be a studio presence. Critics said that when Yoko was around Lennon might have lost his musical edge. Not quite: the Elephants saw a man serious about his craft and not always tolerant of distractions, no matter the source.

Early rehearsals featured Lennon showing chords and arrangements to the group. Lennon sat at the piano; Yoko shared the bench as he ran through "Imagine." He played the introduction and began singing. Yoko interrupted with a word of advice.

Lennon stopped playing and politely asked Yoko to be quiet. He started playing again, and within seconds was interrupted by his wife.

"Please," Lennon said. "Just let me show the guys the song, okay?"

He started again, and the inevitable happened. On the third interruption, Lennon's fingers slowed neither a beat nor a measure in their playing.

"Yoko, shut the fuck up," Lennon said, and finished the song.

The Elephants learned that Lennon's life was far more complicated than what they read in magazines or saw on television. In the aftermath of the Beatles there were endless assumptions made about Lennon's relationship with Paul McCartney, tales that had them either ready to reunite or at each other's throats, depending upon the day and mood.

"You heard a different rumor every other week that they were getting back together," Gary Van Scyoc says. "It wasn't going to happen then. But I didn't really sense any animosity between John and Paul. At the Record Plant, Paul would call on the phone and the session would stop and they'd talk for an hour and a half. Then you'd see an article the next day about how they hated each other."

The Elephants were not expected to be McCartney-caliber collaborators, but Lennon sought input from the musicians. Gabriel was amazed when Lennon requested feedback while writing songs for *Some Time in New York City.*

"He really wanted an opinion," Gabriel says. "Here he was, this rhythmic genius, but he didn't stick that in your face. His ego was really in check. If anything, I think he was more insecure than a lot of celebrities."

Lennon wanted to work with, not necessarily guide, the musicians, and treated the Elephants with professional respect. What surprised Gabriel most was how relaxed Lennon made the bandsmen feel, and how the barely twenty-one-year-old Gabriel felt in Lennon's company.

"I can really look back and see how far out it was to have that natural comfort with someone of that magnitude," Gabriel says. "I mean, there I was learning a tune, and he's asking: 'Do you like it?' I never felt like, 'This is John Lennon the Beatle, what am I doing here?' You felt you belonged there. He made you feel that way."

Lennon relaxed during such times with the group, ending

work sessions with late dinners or at Bank Street; quiet, low-key times that allowed—at least in Lennon's mind—the illusion of anonymity.

"It was cool not to be too in awe of him," says Prewitt. "It was cooler to just walk the street, 'Oh, hey John, how ya doing?' Occasionally there would be people outside the studio, but never big crowds. He felt really comfortable there."

Sometimes that same innocent attitude clouded Lennon's vision. After a recording session ended in the predawn hours, Van Scyoc was driving uptown when he spotted John and Yoko by themselves on an Eighth Avenue corner trying to hail a taxi.

"What the hell are you doing?" he yelled. "Get the hell in the car!" He couldn't believe they hadn't arranged a driver, or weren't aware of the boundaries they crossed—regardless of their celebrity—in a neighborhood populated mostly by "derelicts and prostitutes" at that hour.

"But they loved New York so much they thought nothing about walking down Eighth to catch a cab," Van Scyoc says. "They thought they were totally incognito and nobody would notice, but that's just not the way it was."

•   •   •

SUSPICIONS ABOUT JOHN Lennon had been aired in the Oval Office prior to Strom Thurmond's early February memo suggesting deportation. A year earlier Nixon had been warned about those troublesome Beatles by the King of Rock and Roll, Elvis Presley.

The landscape of America had changed since Elvis joined

the Army in 1958; at the time Presley was clearly the top name in the pop universe, and some cynically considered the induction a patriotic career move. If so, the strategy was misguided as Presley never again reached the chart-topping dominance of his early, Sun Records era. After his days in uniform, Presley spent the "Beatlemania" years making formulaic movies that produced a few hit records, but the British invasion, explosion of rock talent, psychedelia, and the passing of time seemed to leave the King and other '50s pioneers behind. Like Nixon, Presley staged a brief comeback in 1968, a leather-clad glimpse of his rock and roll roots before a final career stage of cabaret spectacle, with Vegas neon reflected off his sequined jumpsuit.

Among other hobbies, Presley developed a fondness for law enforcement and collected guns, badges, and honorary titles from police agencies. Presley was sincere in his concern for his country, and in December 1970 reached out to the president of the United States to offer his assistance.[4]

While sharing first-class airline space with Senator George Murphy (a California Republican and show business veteran of movie musicals including *For Me and My Gal*), Presley wrote a letter that was delivered to Nixon. The nation faced enemies from within, according to Elvis, dissident elements that trusted him in ways that conventional investigators couldn't achieve. Presley offered to be the highest-profile spy since Marlene Dietrich vamped for the Allies: "The drug culture, the hippie elements, the SDS, Black Panthers, etc., do not consider me their enemy or as they call it the establishment. I call it America and I love it. Sir, I can and will be of any service that I can to help my country."

Presley asked to be named a "Federal Agent at Large." He wanted a badge, of course, but not a formal "title or an appointed position." With unintended, tragic irony, Presley said he spoke with authority on the matter: "I have done an in-depth study of drug abuse and Communist brainwashing techniques and I am right in the middle of the whole thing where I can and will do the most good."

A White House meeting was scheduled. Presley was taken to the Oval Office on the morning of December 21; in preparation for the visit deputy assistant to the president Dwight Chapin advised White House chief of staff H. R. Haldeman that Presley's credibility included a recent award from the Junior Chamber of Commerce (Jaycees): "Presley was voted one of the ten outstanding young men for next year and this was based upon his work in the field of drugs."

The historic meeting began with photographs that, decades later, are described as among the most requested from the National Security Archive's considerable collection: Presley, wearing a velvet cape of sorts under a wingspan collar, enormous belt buckle shimmering amidst the glare, eyes more glassy than seductively sleepy, shook hands with a visibly uncomfortable Richard Nixon.

The Nixon-Presley meeting was summarized in a memorandum, "For the President's File," written by attorney Egil "Bud" Krogh, who had served as Nixon's liaison to the FBI and Bureau of Narcotics and Dangerous Drugs. The first paragraph described introductory small talk. Presley said he was currently headlining in Nevada.

"The President indicated that he was aware of how difficult it is to perform in Las Vegas," Krogh noted. An understanding man, Nixon.

In the second paragraph, Nixon explained his hopes that Presley could help reach young people; Elvis said he did that while singing. They both agreed that Elvis should maintain his credibility with America's youth.

Then they discussed the Beatles. The third paragraph begs the question of Elvis's own paranoid tendencies: "Presley indicated that he thought the Beatles had been a real force for anti-American spirit. He said the Beatles came to this country, made their money, and then returned to England where they promoted an anti-American theme. The President nodded in agreement and expressed some surprise."

The heavy-drinking president and prescription-loaded singer then spoke of America's enemies within. "The President indicated that those who use drugs are also those in the vanguard of anti-American protest," Krogh wrote, echoing the White House philosophy that opposition to the war was unpatriotic. "Violence, drug usage, dissent, protests all seem to merge in generally the same group of young people."

Some people wondered, based on the report and photo, if Elvis was under the influence of various pills at the time. Krogh made several references to Presley's emotional state: passionately telling the president he was "on your side"; humbly saying he was "just a poor boy from Tennessee" who'd been blessed by America and wanted to return the favor. At meeting's end Presley repeated his support for Nixon, "and then, in a surprising, spontaneous gesture, put his left arm around the president and hugged him."

Presley's embrace of the president—symbolically and literally—ranks among the most awkward moments in Oval Office history. The legendary meeting ended inconclusively. Gifts were exchanged: a faux Bureau of Narcotics and Dangerous Drugs badge for Presley; a commemorative World War II–era Colt .45 pistol joined the Nixon arsenal ("encased in a handsome wooden chest," according to the thank-you note). Elvis continued sweating it out on Vegas stages, and little or no evidence exists that he made any headway in infiltrating the hippies, SDS, or Black Panther Party.

Many insiders maintain that Nixon was sincere in his attempts to communicate with the young, to find common ground with those who so actively loathed him. Efforts to reach across the generational divide included a 1968 campaign-year cameo on *Laugh-In,* when Nixon delivered the "sock it to me" catchphrase as a question rather than invitation. It was no secret that Nixon wasn't always comfortable in social settings.

"He was clumsy with people," says Joseph Blatchford, Nixon's 1969 appointee as director of the Peace Corps. Blatchford recalls the president sometimes trying odd methods of connecting with young people, including an early morning Lincoln Memorial visit with protestors who had flocked to DC after Kent State. Accompanied by just a single aide, Nixon climbed the steps of the memorial and truly freaked out the hippies who awoke to a private audience with the president of the United States.

"It was a bizarre thing to do," Blatchford says, especially at a time when the White House was prepared to go on lockdown status if post–Kent State demonstrations took a turn for the worse. "He was troubled and he tried to talk to them." Nixon stopped short of asking the kids about their favorite subjects in school as he struggled to make conversation, bringing up football and

surfing, among other topics. Travel, the president advised the
young, was a good way to broaden one's mind.

From Blatchford's perspective, international trips were a deli-
cate topic. He'd been warned that Peace Corps volunteers should
not be wandering the globe and bad-mouthing the president
or the nation's defense policy. "The Vietnam War really split
up the country badly," Blatchford says. The Peace Corps mostly
attracted idealistic youth fresh from college. "They were torn:
they desired to take Kennedy's call and go overseas and serve
and, at the same time, were coming out of college where all the
campuses were saying no, stay here and fight Nixon and the war."

In spite of the seeming divide, with Nixon seen as top antag-
onist, Blatchford says the president had a soft spot for the young
generation, however ill-expressed, that was sometimes revealed.
"I was surprised when he told me he was all for the eighteen-
year-old vote," Blatchford says. "I was trying to encourage him to
move forward with it. Others in the administration said it would
cost him the '72 election. He said, 'I don't care, I think they
should have the vote.'"

Blatchford says Nixon himself supported the Peace Corps and
its mission; others would have preferred ending the program after
the Kennedy administration. One notable problem involved Peace
Corps volunteers who took part in antiwar protests. Blatchford
stood his ground admirably in the face of considerable pressure.

"I had some dealings with the White House, some unpleasant
ones," Blatchford recalls. "Strangely enough, I got most of my
support from Nixon himself. Vice President Agnew got all upset
and wanted me to fire these people."

Blatchford struggled to keep the corps neutral and met resistance from both sides of the aisle. After Kennedy the agency became part of the government, which made it vulnerable to politics.

"Nixon was very positive, but not so much some of his aides. They wanted to go after the young guys with long hair. It was tense."

However superficial, hair length was very much a barometer of the decade's conflicts, fashion attributed to rock and roll and certain bands in particular. In the early 1960s, Blatchford was a Berkeley law student and founder of global-action group Accion. He visited London just as the times began-a-changing.

"I'd never seen young men with long hair before, [or heard of them] except in Shakespeare's time," Blatchford says. "And here were these guys on the street with long hair and funny suits imitating the Beatles. That was the first time I saw the youth antiestablishment message, before I saw it in this country and before the Vietnam War became a big issue."

By 1972 the war in Southeast Asia was the most telling symptom of the national condition. The confusion in Washington was matched by uncertainty throughout the land, which Blatchford said included journalists and activists.

"There was an attempt in society, fanned by the media, where people were trying to get a fight going," Blatchford says. "It was hard to figure out who were the dangerous guys, who were the criminals, who were the saints and spiritual leaders. It was a very confusing time."

Confusion, as with politics, made for strange bedfellows, and Blatchford says that many well-meaning people may have

stepped into situations ill prepared. No one, including Elvis
Presley and John Lennon, knew quite what to make of the Black
Panthers, often perceived as a militant threat.

"A lot of naïve people got involved with some very dangerous
characters," Blatchford says. "I remember Leonard Bernstein giving a fundraiser for the Black Panthers. It was a time of liberation
for women, for blacks, and the whole racial thing going on, and
at the same time there was the voice of Martin Luther King."

In February 1972, Blatchford himself was on the same roster as
Black Panther Party cofounder Bobby Seale, among others, in a
decidedly unexpected forum.

"Mike Douglas turned the show over to him for a week,"
Blatchford says. "Lennon asked for me to come on the show; he
wanted to hear about volunteerism and so forth."

•　　•　　•

MIKE DOUGLAS FOUND his days with Lennon to be memorable for many reasons, describing their time together as "one of
the most interesting, most trying and, in the end, most reward-
ing week of shows we ever produced."

Add "unprecedented" and "unusual" to that description. For
Douglas, having John and Yoko as his cohosts for five one-hour
installments of his talk and variety program was obviously a
show business and ratings coup. In his memoir, *I'll Be Right Back*,
Douglas considered the Beatles "the most sought-after guests
in the entertainment world," an opportunity he was "determined not to waste."[5] If certain allowances had to be made to

accommodate the whims of the guest hosts, Douglas knew it was a small price to pay.

It was customary for Douglas to offer his weekly cohosts a chance to bring on guests of their choosing, "but never to the extent that we did for John and Yoko."

Lennon had a few visitors in mind, names more likely heard on the evening news than on an afternoon talk show. Viewers expected from these shows nothing more than family friendly comedians, middle-of-the-road ballads, and favorite recipes shared during cooking demonstrations. Douglas, a former big-band singer who provided Prince Charming's vocals in *Cinderella*, called his easygoing ambitions "an enjoyable way to pass part of the afternoon watching television and sell some soap." (The genial Douglas said that with false modesty: he was a quiet champion of civil rights and during the early 1960s featured more black leaders than any show on national television at the time. A network memo called Douglas out for having "an excess of Negro activists that may not be appropriate for our daytime audience," and Douglas responded by inviting to the show Stokely Carmichael, the Trinidad-born "honorary prime minister" of the Black Panther Party credited with popularizing the term "black power.")

Of course, Carmichael hadn't been recently convicted of starting a riot, as had two of John and Yoko's wish list of invitees, Jerry Rubin and Bobby Seale. Lennon's broad range of interests and recently made friends resulted in a wildly diverse cast from the worlds of entertainment and politics. Some of the ideas fell short—Lennon had hoped to bring Secretary of State Henry

Kissinger and Groucho Marx to the party—but the assembled cast guaranteed a week of television history: Washington-based names included Joseph Blatchford from the Peace Corps and consumer advocate Ralph Nader, whose 1965 auto industry exposé *Unsafe at Any Speed* ushered in a new era of safety watchdogging; comedy came courtesy of George Carlin, who had recently dropped the suit-and-tie approach in favor of long hair and social commentary. The eclectic atmosphere was complete with Yoko Ono art demonstrations, a civil rights attorney, and a macrobiotic cooking expert sharing space with conventional guests such as veteran TV comic Louis Nye.

Advance guest list negotiations gave the bandsmen of Elephant's Memory their first up-close look at the level of clout held by Lennon.

"The fact that Mike Douglas would do anything to have John on his show is a testament to who John was as a musical icon," Adam Ippolito says. "There were a number of major debates over some of the guests before the show started taping; he even had Eldridge Cleaver on the list if I remember correctly."

"Those people were a condition that John gave," Tex Gabriel says. "I don't see Mike Douglas calling for Bobby Seale on his own."

In turn, John and Yoko felt that some of the conventional guests had been forced on them. Lennon vented in a letter to friend Pete Bennett, an American public relations man working at Apple Records: "I don't know whether you heard of all the problems we've had with the people on Mike Douglas's show? They keep trying to spring 'surprise guests' on us, and we can hardly control them. We don't see much chance of getting you on the show—we can only just get the people we originally wanted on! They fight us every step of the way!"[6]

Musically, the show introduced Elephant's Memory in their new role as Lennon's backup band. *The Daily News* made note of the group's recent promotion "after a long, crazy underground life making music without ever making it as an overground name."[7]

Anticipation was high: the musicians prepared to share a national stage with a Beatle; Rubin delighted in turning a mainstream entertainment program into a Yippie forum; and Douglas recalled a frantic buildup as he and his Philadelphia staff and crew prepared for a week that "drew more interest from disparate groups of people than any other show in our history." Executives from sponsor Westinghouse made appearances on a set they hadn't seen in years; relatives of Douglas and the staff suddenly decided a visit to Philadelphia was long overdue.

Douglas was also aware of "at least a half dozen conservatively dressed men in attendance every day," later confirmed to be FBI agents who were sent "to keep an eye on the suspiciously radical Beatle."

•   •   •

EACH DAY, THE *Mike Douglas Show* began with a song, something perhaps appropriate for the cohost. In the case of Lennon, Douglas opened the Monday, February 14, show with a well-intended if ill-chosen selection.

The stage had been set, the cast in place while an announcer welcomed the studio audience and America to the day's show. Douglas held a microphone onstage and performed the day's first number.

"In the wings, I'm standing beside John," Gary Van Scyoc says. "The show begins and all of a sudden we hear Mike Douglas singing 'Michelle.'"

Douglas or his staff failed to recognize that the Lennon-McCartney byline on Beatles compositions was often deceptive; many songs were effectively solo pieces, such as Lennon's "In My Life" and "Strawberry Fields Forever," or McCartney creations including "Yesterday" and "Michelle." The music hall melody, French verse, and floating vocal of "Michelle" were very much the work of Paul McCartney, and not necessarily one of Lennon's favorites.

Lennon shook his head. "Fuckin' hell," he scowled.

"You could hear somebody's face drop," Van Scyoc says. "John couldn't believe it. He was totally nervous anyway, going on television for millions of people, but Mike comes out and does a Paul song. Just a terrible way to start the week."

The viewing audience—the studio crowded with friends-of-friends, Beatles fans, and FBI agents, plus millions of housewives at home—was unaware that Lennon had been spewing a string of curses moments before he strode onstage. Always the pro, Lennon accepted Douglas's gracious introduction, which may have made matters worse by crediting Lennon for the composition.

John and Yoko appeared on cue, smiled, and shook hands with Douglas while the audience cheered. The central stage area featured an arc of seats for Douglas and his guests, and John and Yoko made themselves comfortable before their microphones. Lennon gently made note of the true authorship of "Michelle," and allowed that he did help write part of the song, just to make Douglas feel better.[8]

After the introductions Lennon offered a simple yet broad statement as keynote for the week: "We'd like to talk about love, peace, communicating, women's lib, racism, war. That's what's going on now."

The first day's guests included Ralph Nader, whom Lennon introduced as "the kind of guy who sets an example, he does something." When asked by Lennon about any political plans, Nader said he would "not ever" be interested in running for president, even though Lennon volunteered his service as minister of music.

The hour went easily with performances by the Chambers Brothers and Louis Nye, John and Yoko sang "It's So Hard," and Yoko exhibited two interactive art pieces whose titles were self-explanatory: *Mending a Broken Teacup* and *Reach Out and Touch Someone in the Audience*. Douglas had no preshow concerns about the first day's talk or topics, and thought the episode went well.

But the following day was not one that Douglas looked forward to, not with a guest list that included a man he described as "an unrepentant anarchist."

Before Jerry Rubin was brought onstage, Douglas explained his reservations: "My feelings are quite negative about this young man. But John wanted him on the show."

Ever the diplomat, Lennon introduced Rubin by

acknowledging that he understood the reputation of the Chicago Seven and the Movement's hard-core radicals; he, too, had wondered if they were "bomb-throwing freaks" to be avoided.

"When I first met Jerry Rubin I was terrified," Lennon said. On the other hand, Lennon had a soft spot for people who may have been misrepresented in the press, having been subjected to that once or twice: "We thought we'd give them a chance to show what they think now, not two years ago or three years ago, and what their hopes are for the future. They do represent a certain part of the youth. I think it's time they spoke themselves."

Which Rubin did, and confirmed Douglas's worst fears by immediately launching into anti-Nixon rants. He blamed the president for creating an automated war, "so that it's machines killing people," and claimed that Nixon's storm-trooper mentality was demonstrated at Attica and Kent State.

Lennon interviewed Rubin on the "Movement," and where it stood. Rubin said that the cause was more necessary than ever "because the repression is so heavy that anyone who does anything gets arrested, jailed, killed."

Douglas interrupted: "This is the only country in the world where a man can say something like that on television."

Rubin said he himself faced prison time for speaking his mind, for saying the harsh truths that needed to be heard. Douglas changed the subject to one that he hoped would shine a more positive light, a topic that was agreed upon before the broadcast. Douglas said he heard Rubin was now against drugs, a reversal of positions.

"That's not true," Rubin responded, mugging for the cameras

and audience. "I'm not against drugs; just heroin." According to Jerry Rubin, heroin was a tool employed by the police to keep minorities in their place.

"He just got on my nerves," Douglas later said, frustrated by Rubin's predictable antigovernment rant.

Lennon steered the conversation toward voting and the need to encourage now-eligible eighteen-year-olds to register and participate. Rubin, of course, said the voting should only be done to remove Nixon, and that young people should vote as a bloc.

After a commercial, Rubin encouraged young people to attend both the Democratic and Republican conventions, "and nonviolently make our presence felt."

"Nonviolently," Lennon repeated the qualifier, although Rubin couldn't resist explaining why nonviolence was the only wise course.

"Because if we do anything any other way we'll be killed," Rubin said. "That's the kind of country we live in."

The audience was not of the same mind, and responded with some booing, catcalls, and jeering; the gentle talk show atmosphere turned tense. Lennon tried to tone things down as he had the David Frost conversation about Attica. "Everybody's entitled to their opinion," Lennon said. "Whatever is going on, we're all responsible for."

In hindsight, Douglas recognized a born peacemaker. "John picked up the mantle of Kind and Gentle Host and he did it quite well, reinterpreting Jerry's comments to take some of the sting out and adding a little humor to keep things cool."[9]

The Rubin show came and went, an exercise in rhetoric where

few viewpoints were changed, some confirmed. Certainly the FBI agents in the audience took note of a man focused on the removal of a president.

Politics aside, Lennon's personal highlight for the week was on Wednesday, when the former Beatle jammed with rock and roll pioneer Chuck Berry.

"John was just in heaven," Gabriel says. "He'd never worked with Chuck Berry; he was in awe of Berry the way everyone else was in awe of Lennon."

Lennon and the Elephants joined Berry for two songs: "Johnny B. Goode," one of the cornerstone riffs that made the electric guitar rock and roll's instrument of choice, and "Memphis." Like Lennon, Berry had his own stubborn, defiant streak. Van Scyoc says some adjustments were needed when Berry began the song differently than he had in rehearsal.

"He proceeded to do the song in his key, even after we all agreed on what key to play in," Van Scyoc says. "John wasn't very happy. The look he gave when we started the song said it all. We were in a panic, not only performing live on national television but starting in the wrong key. I thought we did a good job; John was straining a little with his voice because of that."

Another voice caught Berry by surprise during "Memphis." The first verse went fine. When the chorus came around, the background singing included Yoko's unique, piercing vocalizations. Berry's eyes popped wide for a moment, but the veteran entertainer took it on the chin and continued unfazed.

A close-up captured Berry sharing the microphone for a duet with Lennon, whose smile summed up the experience. No matter the radical politics of the week, John Lennon's heart was captured in those few minutes. Douglas said a grinning Lennon told him that, no matter what else, playing with Berry was "worth the whole gig, eh?"

Yet it was a guest on the fourth episode who provided the most nervous anticipation of the week: it was time for the housewives to meet a Black Panther. Douglas, hardly a stranger to the civil rights movement, admitted that his audience might not have been ready for some guests.

"After the trying experience with Jerry Rubin, I was hardly looking forward to Bobby Seale," Douglas said. "The public viewed the Black Panthers as heavily armed, white-hating militants. Talk about the perfect way to alienate my core viewing audience."

Douglas expected attitude from a man likely to use the word "pigs" to describe police officers or phrases such as "up against the wall" to raise militant anger. Instead, Douglas heard descriptions of Panther clothing drives, breakfast programs for inner-city students, and other community-based activism.

Lennon explained that when he met the Panther leader he was surprised by what he learned.

"He had a lot to say," Lennon said. "He's doing a lot that was not what I'd read in the paper about him. The Foundation, giving food to people, the programs of education . . . and we thought, well, let's see that side of these people."

Seale discussed the Panthers' ten-point program, a controversial doctrine yet one that contained a philosophy of empowerment and local responsibility.

Douglas readily admitted his surprise, and pleasure: "All I can say is, God bless Bobby Seale. There was no trace of the rancor I expected." Douglas welcomed Seale's descriptions of programs to collect shoes for the needy, and film clips showed the Panthers giving out bags of groceries. What was said seemed less important than how it was presented—with civility and genuine passion.

By week's end, Douglas realized "the headaches were minor," and the respect he held for Lennon the musician was matched by his assessment of the man. "He was smart, funny, gregarious, and beguiling," Douglas said. "He was as good a listener as a talker, with a genuine compassion for other people and respect for other philosophies."

As a bonus, Douglas was given a look at what some still considered the mystery of the ages: "I came to understand something about John's affection for this woman," Douglas said of Yoko Ono. "She was strange and could be difficult, but she was a powerful character."

Throughout the week Yoko showcased her music and art, including telephoning random numbers and telling whoever answered, "We love you," or what Douglas called a "baffling" piece, a mirror-lined box for people to hold and grin at themselves. "Collecting smiles" was the concept, and Yoko passed the box around for all to try.

"John turned to me and said, 'I live with her and I still don't get a lot of this stuff,'" Douglas recalled. "You had to like the guy."

Not everyone appreciated Yoko. People who adored John, including fans and colleagues, often made her the scapegoat for the Beatles' breakup and Lennon's seemingly strange stunts like the bed-ins or bagism. She was perhaps an easy target for critics, and the bandsmen saw some who took advantage of that. Rehearsals for Yoko's singing performances generated harsh laughter and comments from the show's crew.

"She was crying during rehearsal," Ippolito says. "That had to be smoothed over."

Yoko wore a brave broadcast face even when—as legend has it—the crew kept her microphone muted during musical segments. Ippolito recognized that, as a musician, Lennon may have given her the benefit of the doubt, a case of the things you do for love.

"He knew what she sounded like," Ippolito says. "He was also into freedom of expression and art, and was taken by her mystique."

Yoko Ono was a woman of mystery, which may have been Joseph Blatchford's assessment after they shared a stage. Blatchford was largely unaware of Lennon's politics and knew the man primarily for his art. "I had not followed him much other than as a musician with the Beatles," Blatchford says. "It came up during the show."

On air, Lennon interviewed Blatchford about volunteerism. What the audience may not have seen was Blatchford's exchange with Yoko during a commercial break. Blatchford recalls Yoko, polite and friendly, discreetly taking his hand.

"She passed me a note, secretly, written in red pen," Blatchford says. "Her personal phone number; and she either wrote or whispered to me that she was looking for help with the authorities for John. She wondered if I could help them."

Blatchford didn't give too much thought to Yoko's request; there really wasn't anything he could do from the humble Peace Corps office. He found Lennon to be "very pleasant and very nice," and thought the show went well.

He soon learned that the Nixon administration put Lennon in the same category as what they considered "provocateurs with secret missions to undermine our security." Given his experience with an increasingly paranoid administration, Blatchford found it sadly believable that a presidential staff would place a musician under surveillance, consider him a threat, and try to force deportation.

"It wouldn't surprise me at all if those guys were saying, 'Let's get the FBI on this guy,'" Blatchford says. "They overdid it."

CHAPTER 4

"A THOROUGH NUISANCE"

"If the man wants to shove us
out
we're gonna jump and shout:
the Statue of Liberty said,
'Come!'"
—JOHN LENNON,
"New York City"

THE NIXON ADMINISTRATION'S attempt to send John Lennon packing began with the US Department of Immigration and Naturalization. On March 1, 1972, the Lennons were informed that their visitor visas would not be renewed, and that they must depart these shores no later than March 15.

A second notice went out just five days later, after the INS district director concluded that the Lennons "had no intention to leave," and they were notified that deportation proceedings would soon begin.[1]

Washington observers believed the matter was settled, and

that the election-motivated "counterstrategy" suggested by Senator Strom Thurmond appeared successful. Thurmond was told by White House aide William Timmons that Lennon wouldn't be around by August convention time. The perceived threat to presidential security had been addressed: "You may be assured the information you previously furnished has been appropriately noted."

The Lennons had several valid reasons for being in the country, the most compelling of which had been so Yoko could be near her daughter, Kyoko, who was in the custody of her former husband Tony Cox. Beginning in early 1971 John and Yoko had made several trips to America seeking clarification on parental rights from Texas courts; both Cox and Kyoko were US citizens believed to have a Houston residency. Yoko's custody quest sparked thoughts of making America their home, hand-in-hand with Lennon's need to distance himself from London bitterness in his post-Beatles world.

Attorney Leon Wildes says that renewing passport papers should have been a relatively routine matter, and the family issue alone qualified for extensions. "I was surprised by the whole thing," Wildes says. "They really weren't asking for much."

Wildes had been a law school classmate of Alan Kahn, who served as house counsel to Apple Records. When Lennon, one of Apple's founding artists, was served with deportation papers, Kahn thought first of Wildes & Weinberg, among the best and most INS-experienced firms in New York. He called his old friend to offer him the case, and was amazed by Wildes's first question: "Alan, tell me, who is John Lennon?"

"Never admit that you asked me that question," Kahn advised.

Born and raised in a small Pennsylvania town, Wildes was more familiar with classical music and his beloved opera than contemporary music styles. While it's difficult to imagine living in New York City through the late '60s unaware of Lennon and the Beatles, Wildes instead viewed John and Yoko as he did the East-West romance in Verdi's *Aida*.

"I didn't know who John Lennon and Yoko Ono were," Wildes says. "I knew even less about their music. I just saw a beautiful couple, a beautiful marriage that seemed to go beyond the usual. When I found out who they were, how important they were, I grew to appreciate it even more."

Wildes went to Bank Street for an initial consultation. Most guests hung out in laid-back fashion in the largest room—space organized around a central bed and sprinkled with guitars and peace signs like any groovy Village pad, except for the Academy Award (*Let It Be*) on a crowded bookshelf—but business was business and the Lennons paid due courtesies to the attorney. "They came out to a back room, and that was kind of a respectful stand," Wildes says.

Wildes appreciated John and Yoko's desire to remain in America, and assured them that Yoko's need to have access to her daughter—with her husband at her side—made a compelling legal argument.

There was one possible problem: Lennon traveled with the baggage of a 1968 misdemeanor conviction for possession of cannabis. Sergeant Norman Pilcher and the London Drug Squad had arrested Lennon as part of a series of pop-star busts; Pilcher's

mug shots included George Harrison, Donovan, and no fewer
than three Rolling Stones—Mick Jagger, Keith Richards, and
Brian Jones. On advice of counsel Lennon had pleaded guilty to a
misdemeanor charge and paid a small fine.[2]

That conviction was a relatively minor stain on a passport
application, but technically enough to cancel a visa. During previous visits Lennon had obtained a waiver for temporary stays,
but John and Yoko now wanted more time in America, perhaps
another year; Lennon had been told that the conviction could be
dismissed after five years, and could clear the way for more permanent arrangements. Lennon asked if Wildes could somehow
get them just a little more time.

A grace period should be easy enough, Wildes said. Even better, why not apply for permanent residency?

"If you're as important as everyone says you are," Wildes told
Lennon, "I may be able to put the government in a very embarrassing public posture." Wildes knew that the INS preferred to avoid
trials that involved famous names. INS district director Sol Marks—
who had shared more than a few Long Island Rail Road commutes
with his friend Wildes—and lead prosecutor Vincent Schiano
handled cases ranging from mob bosses to Xaviera Hollander,
author of *The Happy Hooker*. (Hollander reportedly sent Schiano a
copy of her book, in which her inscription asked if he really thought
she was an "undesirable" alien.) Going after Lennon would invite
considerable media exposure; Marks could only imagine the public
backlash if he tried to kick a Beatle out of the country.[3]

Wildes planned to argue that Lennon was an "outstanding
person in the arts or sciences," and challenge the harsh result of

asking a woman to choose between staying with her daughter or leaving with her husband. Informally, Marks told Wildes that an extension of one or two months would likely be granted; but only one, no more.

Marks's response suggested to Wildes there was more to the matter than he thought: "Don't ask me any questions," he told Wildes. "These people will never get another extension. And Leon: tell them to get out."

•　　•　　•

ANOTHER PROTEST BRIEFLY caught Lennon's attention in early March, one inspired by profit rather than politics. Lennon had more than a casual interest at stake; the players involved included a business partner, a fellow former Beatle, and a rock legend.

Allen Klein, a fireball attorney and sometime rock impresario, had been entrusted by Lennon, George Harrison, and Ringo Starr to represent the Beatles post-breakup. (That choice was at odds with Paul McCartney's idea of having his in-laws manage the Apple holdings.) Anointed by three-quarters of the band to handle their affairs, Klein had worked with Lennon on the *Imagine* promotional film, and in 1971 produced Harrison's massive charity benefit, the June "Concert for Bangladesh" at Madison Square Garden. The crisis-driven humanitarian blowout—said to be the first of its kind on such a scale with a superstar cast that included George and Ringo, Eric Clapton, and Bob Dylan—seemed successful at first: millions of relief dollars were generated by concert attendance, record sales, and film rights.

A closer look at the accounting, however, called into question Klein's credibility and the extent of aid actually realized by the show: A February 28, 1972, *New York* magazine article revealed that the bulk of donated funds never made it to Bangladesh. Some went straight to Klein's pockets.[4] A. J. Weberman, a Greenwich Village character and self-declared activist, seized the opportunity for righteous anger and populist protest. Weberman recalls that Klein had employed some creative accounting that was legal if unethical.

"Allen Klein claimed that 85 percent was used for expenses," Weberman says. There were no legal requirements as to a certain percentage of donations making it to the recipient, and Klein's answer gave the impression that he had taken money intended for those in critical need.

"I decided that if he needed to rip off the starving people of Bangladesh, he must be one hungry gentleman," Weberman says. "We decided to have a free lunch program for starving music executives based on the Black Panther breakfast programs."

A week after the *New York* article appeared, Weberman and "a bunch of hippies" stopped by several fruit stands, did some dumpster diving, and took a supply of spoiled produce to Klein's office building; the "free lunch" they deserved, delivered as promised.

"We started trashing his office with rotten fruit," Weberman recalls. A confrontation followed, with arguments over who was helping or hurting the children of Bangladesh. Outside of the office, Weberman claims to have had a sidewalk showdown with producer Phil Spector, who had supervised the Bangladesh recordings.

"I told him I was gonna punch him in the nose and he wouldn't be able to snort coke anymore," Weberman says.

The confrontation had little impact on a matter that took years to resolve. Several lawsuits followed before rights and royalties were straightened out. Ongoing sales of the album, CD, video, and DVD continued into the twenty-first century to benefit the George Harrison Fund for UNICEF.

Weberman enjoyed brief counterculture credibility after taking on the suit-and-tie crowd. Tales were told on the street, in the *Village Voice*, and through the underground grapevine before reaching the ears of John Lennon. Klein's credibility was obviously important to Lennon—the relationship was not fated to be long-term—and any controversy over the Bangladesh concert qualified as a dodged bullet: Lennon had considered joining his former bandmates onstage.

Weberman was invited to Bank Street, "after they heard what we did," he says, and enjoyed talking with John and Yoko about "religion, atheism, politics, the third world, national liberation, the Vietnam War, topics of that nature. Lennon was quite responsive, and we were basically on the same page at the time. We were friends."

John and Yoko indulged Weberman at first, and paid for a postage meter to distribute his *Yippie Times* newspaper; the Lennon/Rubin connection included having Elephant's Memory play at a "Smoke-In," a festival Weberman recalls for a ten-foot-long stage prop: "We rolled this giant joint out of straw at the band shell in Central Park."

It was a brief alliance, one of many fleeting encounters during Lennon's nascent months in Greenwich Village. Lennon willingly met with anyone and everyone; some of those he met then claimed strong relationships after only slightly making John's acquaintance. Weberman had a minor reputation somewhere between cultural critic and curious crackpot, known for stunts in some ways similar to the Yippie model, and for a brand of psychological research he called "garbology," the study of someone's trash to uncover their true nature.

Of particular fascination to Weberman were the garbage cans of Bob Dylan. Weberman stalked Dylan long before that term was coined, and had drawn speculative conclusions from his findings. He declared himself head of the "Dylan Liberation Front" out of concern that the voice of a generation was a drug addict. Weberman claimed that his garbage-can investigations revealed indications of heroin use—which Dylan had reportedly wrestled with briefly—although the science was hardly credible given the recreational residue that might be found in Village trash cans, whether or not generated by the resident. Weberman also believed that Dylan's political loyalties were driven by a need for drugs. In Weberman's view, Dylan was not the liberal voice many believed.

"I had come to the conclusion that Dylan was once a leftist and sold out in order to take heroin and make a lot of money," Weberman says. "I was wrong: he was never a leftist, he was always on the right to begin with."

That's where Weberman lost Lennon, who considered Dylan a friend, a songwriting influence, and pioneer messenger of New Left ideals.

"Lennon and I had our differences about Bob Dylan,"

Weberman acknowledges. "If I said something bad about Dylan, he got really agitated and Yoko had to hold him back. People hated me when I went after Dylan. Everybody loved John, and if you loved John you hated Weberman."

When he went after Allen Klein, Weberman said his actions were on behalf of the Rock Liberation Front—yet another name to confuse federal investigators—an organization he said had evolved from his own Dylan Liberation Front. His claim that John and Yoko were the newest RLF soldiers had already been publicly denied in a *Village Voice* letter from the true Rock Liberation Front, which consisted of the Lennons, Rubin, and David Peel.[5] They denounced Weberman for his Dylan obsession and wild accusations, and deplored the tendency within the Left of attacking one another: "A. J. Weberman's campaign . . . is in the current fad of everyone in the revolution attacking each other and spreading false rumors about each other."

There had been more than enough of that in Lennon's life already by that point.

•   •   •

WAS JOHN LENNON merely a means to an end for his new friends in the Movement, a bit player in an ongoing political game, or had he assumed a more powerful role? FBI reports in March 1972 struggled to clarify Lennon's place in the Movement, the leadership of which seemed to be in transition. Undercover agents, informants, and investigators pooled information from sources both credible and inflated.

By then Jerry Rubin's populist act had eclipsed his usefulness in the eyes of many of his former friends in the Movement. After his embarrassing performance on the *Mike Douglas Show*, Rubin was questioned about—among other things—his outrageous statements that did more to harm than help the cause. In a March 5 report, FBI informant Julie Maynard described a recent gathering of Yippie leaders in Rubin's Prince Street apartment. The report did not specify everyone involved in the leadership intervention, but noted that Chicago Seven vet Stew Albert was among the participants. The session began with Rubin complaining that his so-called friends were responsible for the "bad press" he'd been getting lately, which "hurt him politically."[6]

Rather than the hoped-for sympathy, Rubin was called onto his own carpet.

"They replied that they thought he was an asshole," Maynard said of the response. The group proceeded to list their "bitches" with Rubin: He wasn't a team player, and he had profited financially while theoretically raising funds for the cause. He had "a superstar ego which enables him to appear to lead . . . he does none of the work yet gets the credit." As a final thought, Rubin was chastised on a personal level for "his b.o. and other bad habits."

Rubin had not only lost the respect of his colleagues on the Left, they also wondered if his reputation-saving trump card was still valid: word on the street said that Rubin's friendship with John Lennon had ended. Lennon's once-assured participation in an upcoming rally—let alone the August convention— was now a tentative commitment that came with qualifications. Lennon insisted on low-key involvement, and would not go along with Rubin's any-means-necessary strategies for civil disobedience.

The FBI now realized that Lennon was more than just a "drawing card" to be played at Rubin's discretion; more like a wild card. Investigators didn't seem to know from one day to the next where Lennon stood with the radicals or what his actual plans were, and their reports varied in accuracy and credibility. One dispatch said that the Lennon-fronted concert tour was ready to start, "the first to be held in Ann Arbor Michigan in near future." By "near future" they may have meant several months earlier: the Michigan show was old news by then, as was Lennon's relationship with the Detroit hippies; the report incorrectly suggested that Lennon and John Sinclair were working together to plan the August showdown.

Another point of uncertainty offered a possible method to force Lennon's departure, if reports of his drug use were accurate. A March 16 summary suggested that Rennie Davis, Rubin, and Lennon were "heavy users of narcotics," and that the three were at odds with each other because of their unspecified drug use. Lennon's consumption was said to be "excessive" and included pills "referred to in the vernacular as 'downers,'" although specifics on that score varied. The memo dismissed Lennon's passion for protest on the basis that he was too stoned to care: "Lennon appears to be radically oriented, however he does not give the impression he is a true revolutionist since he is constantly under the influence of narcotics."

There are varying accounts on Lennon's actual drug use—and he was certainly no virgin to the drink, pills, hallucinogens, and even narcotics that had been tried by most of his contemporaries.

At one extreme Lennon had admittedly tried heroin, and sang of withdrawal in "Cold Turkey." Yet some unflattering biographies painted an exaggerated portrait of Lennon spending weeks at a time in drug-induced stupor—supposedly during periods when he maintained a rigorous schedule and was making credible public appearances. Elephant's Memory bandsmen recall a time and place where smoking a joint was as casual as having a drink, but claim that Lennon fell far short of rendering himself unable to function. They all saw—and would sadly continue to see—too many of those types of cases not to know the difference.

That Lennon used drugs was understood, but to what extent depended upon witness perspective and bias. The FBI may have been simply repeating rumors that the agents heard, but "constantly under the influence" was among many internal contradictions found in field reports, memos, and directives.

There was an equal amount of confusion as to the various organizational names used by the Movement leaders—and their purpose. A collective People's Coalition for Peace and Justice was said to represent more than one hundred "disruptive" groups nationwide; convention plans fell under the watch of the Lennon-funded Election Year Strategy Information Center. These people had a history of "using massive civil disobedience to combat war, racism, poverty and repression."

One thing the FBI reports agreed upon, evidence notwithstanding, was the plan of this particular organization: "To conduct disruptive demonstrations during the Republican National Convention." In spite of the bureau's own report the previous month that quoted Lennon as specifying peaceful—therefore legal—means of protest, J. Edgar Hoover declared that Lennon's plans were not passive, thus allowing further investigation. According to Hoover, Lennon had an "avowed intention to engage in disruptive activities" at the convention.

In turn, the bureau tried to prevent that by any means necessary. If Lennon was the "known drug user" they assumed, agents with evidence of that drug use should promptly report to the New York Police Department for an easy arrest. A subsequent directive informed the home office that the NYPD was "attempting to obtain enough information to arrest both subject and wife Yoko based on PD investigation." And yet no such evidence was forthcoming. Maybe Lennon was more drug-free than some of the rumors suggested.

•   •   •

WORD SPREAD QUICKLY when Lennon and the Elephants began a month's worth of sessions in late February for *Some Time in New York City* at the Record Plant studio on West Forty-Fourth Street. The studio experiences were memorable far beyond the musical adventure for the bandsmen, with near daily reminders of just how famous their new friend John really was. Recording sessions often receive guests or friends of the musicians, but the Elephants were stunned at the variety of people who called on Lennon. Tex Gabriel remembers a visitor who probably wasn't used to politely waiting a few minutes to see someone as she did for Lennon.

"I remember having Jackie Onassis come down to the studio,"

Gabriel says. "That was a big moment for me; I'll never forget that."

A lifelong memory for the Elephants, who learned that time with Lennon was precious, as so many had sought what they casually enjoyed. Working with Lennon brought endless surprises, Gary Van Scyoc says, including time-management and logistical challenges to productivity.

"Talk about distractions," Van Scyoc says. "One night Mick Jagger was there for a couple of hours. Rudolf Nureyev, all these people coming at John for various reasons."

Additionally, Lennon's diplomatic skills were called into play with Phil Spector, contracted to serve as producer. Spector had met the Beatles in 1970 when he had been asked to salvage the scattered *Let It Be* tapes. The legendary producer's signature on certain tracks—notably Lennon's "Across the Universe" and McCartney's "The Long and Winding Road"—had added something new and different to the Beatles' repertoire: the multi-track, multi-instrument "wall of sound" he'd mastered with Tina Turner's "River Deep—Mountain High," the Righteous Brothers' "You've Lost that Lovin' Feelin'," and dozens of other classics.

Spector's reputation as a producer was matched by notoriety for his eccentricities. By the time Spector worked with the Beatles he had become something of a recluse and would only work with A-list musicians; to the Elephants he offered at best a cold shoulder.

"He didn't want anything to do with us," Tex Gabriel says. "He did not want to deal with unknowns, and didn't know why Lennon wasn't working with Clapton. We weren't stars; he liked to work with celebrities."

He met his match with John Lennon; Spector's objections were overruled by one of the few musicians able to trump the producer's clout.

"John just told him how it was gonna be," Gabriel says. "Lennon said, 'These are my guys, they're working with me, and I want you to treat them with respect.' He really liked the band, and John could be very direct and forceful when he needed to be."

Once again, Lennon fulfilled the role of peacemaker, smoothed the bumpy introductions, and told the band not to worry about "Phil and his attitude. He's just here to produce and do what he's gotta do." It was agreed that Spector would be a rare studio presence and instead would work independently with the material as he had with *Let It Be*.

The Elephants began to see the potential genius of this unexpected pairing, of what Lennon had seen in choosing them over all the other bands he could have picked. They were, in fact, John Lennon's full-time band. They had done the Mike Douglas week, were in the studio to record an album, and were told of very tempting possibilities for the year ahead. Lennon was ready for more, and the Elephants were an integral part of the plan.

"John didn't do anything together without us, musically, for that period," Van Scyoc says. "It wasn't like we were a side project. He was talking about a world tour."

That plan, as with other ideas, awaited the outcome of Lennon's immigration status. It also made pinpointing the schedule for rehearsals, recording time, and promotional efforts a bit more vexing than it might have been otherwise.

"They were trying to set up some high-profile things with

John," Van Scyoc says. "And he couldn't do it because of the green card. That was a big part of what was happening. He had that, and the search for Kyoko, and they were always taking off. He wanted Yoko to have his total, 100 percent support."

The hectic schedule often changed at the very last moment. A phone call inviting the band to get together meant little an hour later when they learned that Lennon had flown off to Houston; conversely, unexpected calls to grab their instruments were not uncommon.

"It was just absolutely crazy," Van Scyoc says. "You never knew where they were. You'd get a call, 'Let's rehearse in an hour.' Then there were weeks at a time when they wouldn't be around and we resumed our normal thing. That was his career at that point."

●   ●   ●

THEY WORKED FAST because they had to, and also by artistic design. Recording enough material for an album over several weeks was a relatively short production; Lennon wanted *Some Time in New York City* to have the immediacy of a newspaper, a "concept" album in both content and delivery.

"We're like journalists only we sing about it," he had said to David Frost, and the sessions were approached with deadline urgency as they worked on the tracks. Work typically began at seven p.m., all-nighters that allowed enough time to relax, warm up on the guitars, kick around song ideas. The recording room itself was fairly small, its walls lined with amplifiers bearing paper cups or beer cans. Cushioned cubicle-walls dampened a drum kit; microphone and music stands stood in clusters; guitars dominated the center area. Lennon was the focal point as he explained each song to the band.

Musical familiarity formed during early rehearsals in the Village continued when they recorded tracks. Lennon asked for and welcomed opinions, although he brought to the sessions songs that were mostly formed, his efficiency honed after a decade spent in recording studios. The routine worked well: Lennon sketched a foundation in need of bass-and-drum rhythm, keyboard or lead guitar lines, saxophone work from Stan Bronstein. The Elephants were more than capable of keeping pace with Lennon's range of styles; their own credits spanned an impressive spectrum of rock, blues, jazz, and pop.

Some of the songs had been previewed by Lennon in December: "John Sinclair" and its bluesy backing; "Attica State" and its thumping protest chant; Yoko's feminist cry "Sisters O Sisters" tinted with a reggae accent; and "Luck of the Irish," a pub-worthy sing-along voicing the troubles in Northern Ireland. Additional songs included "Angela," a ballad telling the story of activist Angela Davis and her incarceration; "Sunday, Bloody Sunday," also about the Derry massacre in Ireland; and the autobiographical "New York City," which in classic rock and roll style continued the story told in "The Ballad of John and Yoko." Lennon's chorus shouts of "Que pasa, New York" joined verses that described meeting Rubin and Peel, hearing the Elephants at Max's Kansas City, jamming with the group to old songs, and absorbing all things Manhattan.

A straight-out rocker, some thought "New York City" could have been another hit for Lennon if selected as the first single for the LP. "Such a great song, to this day," Van Scyoc says. "In my opinion one of the best songs on the record."

Instead, Lennon defied convention and expectations. The first song from *Some Time* to vie for radio play reported society's treatment of women; Lennon's feminist ballad invited controversy beginning with its title, "Woman Is the Nigger of the World."

•   •   •

JOHN LENNON'S TAKE on the women's movement may have been puzzling to some old-boy Beatles fans, but feminist leader Gloria Steinem wasn't surprised. Steinem recalls Lennon's history of embracing causes. It was a trait she saw early on; in 1964 she had accepted a *Cosmopolitan* magazine assignment to shadow the Beatles around Manhattan, and the hordes of young women who followed them everywhere they went.

"He seemed to be much less interested in them than the other Beatles," Steinem says. "Perhaps I was biased because I'm a writer, too, but I found him more interesting than the others."

Steinem says she'd "read some writings and realized how imaginative he was. He had a great heritage in cockney, rhyming words; you get a sense of them and they contain meaning in an imaginative way." Steinem disagrees with critics who claim Lennon's earliest work reflected a chauvinistic if not misogynistic man, and says Lennon's 1964 book of prose, *In His Own Write*, reveals a deeper soul.

"It's not antiwoman; it doesn't take on sexism," Steinem says. "It's whimsical and imaginative and humane, so he must have been unusually open."

Contrasting with previous perceptions of Lennon in the early Beatles days—when the band and its entourage were seen as very much a boys' club—Lennon welcomed the rise of feminism and the women's movement, which in the early 1970s was in its heyday. Just as the struggle for black civil rights required white awakening, the feminist movement needed the involvement of men. Lennon, Steinem says, had the strength of his convictions and a willingness to defy stereotypes, to walk a different path on principle: "He was antiwar in a country and a world that sometimes measures masculinity by being aggressive. He was creative, again in a world where men are more rewarded for being aggressive than creative. His life—as well as his work—was and still is a liberating influence for everyone, especially for men."

Lennon credited his awakening to Yoko's influence; she asked to be referred to professionally as "Ms. Ono," with the recently coined hybrid of Miss and Mrs. In turn, Lennon legally added "Ono" to his own name, hardly a common practice for men in the late 1960s or any era. In his 1971 *Red Mole* interview, Lennon said that the feminist movement needed to be part of the New Left agenda, whose male leaders were guilty of sexism even as they accused the establishment of being racist: "We can't have a revolution that doesn't involve and liberate women. It's subtle the way you're taught male superiority. It took me a long time to realize that my maleness was cutting off certain areas for Yoko. She's a red hot liberationist and was quick to show me where I was going wrong, even though it seemed to me that I was just acting naturally. That's why I'm interested to know how people who claim to be radical treat women."

In many ways, Steinem says, the women's movement rose

from the shadows of the antiwar and civil rights movements. There were few opportunities at the battlefront, and female volunteers found themselves taking a backseat to the new-boy network.

"If those movements had been equal for women there probably wouldn't have been a women's movement," Steinem says. "Women were still expected to make coffee and do the mimeographing— there's a word from the past—and provide sex and be supportive."

No matter how solemn the issues being addressed—the need for civil rights and an end to war—Steinem says that a certain percentage of men inevitably degraded women in sexual terms, a difficult if not impossible environment to remain sympathetic. Steinem says the problem was best displayed at an antiwar rally in Washington.

"A woman activist got up onstage speaking against the war," Steinem recalls, "and the veterans yelled, 'Take her off and fuck her.'"

Lennon seemed sincere in his feminist values, and Steinem says she understood his decision to sing about it in a shocking, potentially offensive song. In what may be the first feminist pop song of the late '60s or early '70s to come from a man—Helen Reddy's 1971 "I Am Woman" was the unofficial anthem— "Woman Is the Nigger of the World" was released in April 1972. The title was guaranteed to add to the obstacles facing the record in terms of getting radio airplay and the other mechanisms that might make it a hit. Steinem says the effort was notable in ways other than record sales.

"A very serious and important song," Steinem reflects. "Sometimes in order to get one thing taken seriously you have to compare it to something else that is already taken seriously. Women had been called the 'mule of the world,' but not as a phrase in a song."

As often happened with Lennon, lyrics followed the title statement with both a confirmation and a challenge to white men everywhere: "Yes she is, think about it; do something about it."

•   •   •

ROUND ONE WENT to John and Yoko. The March 16, 1972, hearing at the Department of Immigration and Naturalization concluded with an adjournment until May, giving Leon Wildes time to prepare residence applications and for Lennon to try to have the marijuana conviction expunged.

A recent Texas court ruling that granted Yoko custody of Kyoko largely supported the decision. It was, however, a semi-hollow decision that failed to immediately reunite mother and daughter. The *New York Times* called the victory "a pyrrhic one, for the child and her father, Anthony D. Cox, have vanished." According to Yoko, Cox planned to remain in hiding and wait out the deportation.[7] Other sources believed that Cox recognized a potential payoff: new husbands of ex-wives are rarely welcomed by the former spouse, but a multimillionaire rock star invited certain obvious speculations about Cox's motives.

Justice faced a conundrum: The custody order required that Yoko live in America, leaving the INS burdened with splitting up a family if they deported Lennon. Yoko was certain to be granted semipermanent residency; Lennon appeared ready to fight for his, publicly if necessary. On the steps of the INS building, extension in hand, Lennon held an impromptu press conference.

Journalists weren't the only ones taking notes: "A representative of the FBI," as described in a memo, joined the crowd of "eighty-five reporters including radio and television."[8]

When asked, Lennon told what he believed was the truth. According to the memo, "he inferred the INS was attempting to deport him due to his political ideas and present policy of the US government as to aliens who speak out against the administration."

The battle lines were drawn. From the FBI perspective, Director J. Edgar Hoover seemed frustrated that what he considered a problem—Lennon fronting an anti-Nixon concert—had not been quickly solved.

"Strong possibility looms that subject will not be deported any time soon," Hoover advised in early April. "And will probably be in US at least until [Republican National Convention]."

A summary of where things stood after the hearing was sent to individuals not typically involved in deportation hearings, including US attorney general John Mitchell and White House chief of staff H. R. Haldeman. They were in for a fight: Hoover advised that Lennon was more than capable of financing a lengthy legal challenge, and that the media would gladly tell Lennon's side of the story. John Lennon was hardly the exclusive interest of the underground press or *Rolling Stone*; the man whom the FBI had difficulty obtaining a photograph of was a frequent presence in the *New York Times, Daily News, New York Post*, and countless other publications.

The deportation effort became a public drama, and since the true motivation was supposed to be a secret, the rush to kick Lennon out puzzled many. Support for granting residency came from a growing number of people whose standing in the community demanded attention. On behalf of the city Lennon loved, New York mayor John V. Lindsay was among the first to step forward. Lindsay authored an April letter to INS commissioner Raymond Farrell.[9]

Deporting Lennon would be "a grave injustice," Lindsay said. "I consider it to be very much in the public interest, from the point of view of the citizens of New York as well as the citizens of the Country, that artists of their distinction be granted resident status." Lindsay said he'd met with John and Yoko and was told "of their love for New York City and that they wish to make it their home."

Citing the compelling motivation of a mother wishing to be with her child, Lindsay said "the removal of the Lennons from this Country would be contrary both to the principles of our Country as well as the humanitarian practices which should be implemented by the Department of Immigration."

Lindsay did not address Lennon's marijuana conviction, but instead questioned the true reasons for the harassment. Yes, John and Yoko spoke their mind on the issues of the day, but that alone is not a crime: "If this is the motive underlying the unusual and harsh action taken by the Immigration and Naturalization Service, then it is an attempt to silence constitutionally protected 1st Amendment rights of free speech and association and a denial of the civil liberties of these two people."

Well aware of potential public backlash, Lennon told the *New York Times* that Lindsay's letter was "a beautiful thing," and he hoped "no one would be offended by it." Lennon was prone to speak positively rather than critically. Talking to the press he maintained his political ground but also expressed great admiration for the country he sought to call home, an America he hadn't really seen ... at least not as he would have wished.

"All I'd seen of New York was hotels when I was here as a Beatle," Lennon explained, but he'd grown to love the Village and the life he'd found. He spoke of simple pleasures like coffee ice-cream malts and his desire to see more of America, landmarks like the Grand Canyon or cities such as New Orleans.

Mayor Lindsay's voice was not unique. An announcement at Washington's National Press Club reported the formation of the National Committee for John and Yoko (yet another "organization" that bore watching by those concerned about radical groups). Artist and friend of the Lennons John Hendrix rallied the cause and told a gaggle of Beltway journalists that the true reason for the deportation was Yoko and Lennon's "antiwar stand, their ability to affect the thinking of youth and their support of unpopular beliefs."

Preparing to fight a government clearly out to harass him, Lennon and attorney Leon Wildes welcomed support from an impressive body of notable individuals.[10] Letters from the creative world poured in, prominent and respected names, some either as representatives of the Committee for Artistic Freedom, others independently yet with shared outrage and sympathy: actor Tony Curtis; Dick Cavett; artist Andy Warhol; filmmakers Stanley Kubrick and Elia Kazan; novelists Joyce Carol Oates, Joseph Heller, and John Updike, who said of John and Yoko, "They cannot do this great country any harm, and might do it some good." Composers John Cage and Leonard Bernstein weighed in; Bernstein called Lennon "an important creative force in music." Joan Baez added a handwritten comment to the boilerplate letter: "Keeping people confined to certain areas of the world was one of the reasons we've had six thousand years of war instead of six thousand years of peace." Actress and singer Diahann Carroll wrote, "If an appeal to the ethical or moral position of these freedom loving artists will not move you, perhaps you will give special allowance to Mrs. Lennon's position as a mother and the terrible potential danger that she might lose her child by this action. I beg you to give a favorable answer to Mr. and Mrs. Lennon in this matter."

Support also came from outside of the entertainment world. United Auto Workers chief Leonard Woodcock said, "It would be an outrage and a tragedy for this country if John Lennon and Yoko Ono are deported," and cited Lennon's "clear eloquent commitment to nonviolence, and to participation in action for constructive social change."

Rock and roll was represented by Bob Dylan, in a suitably poetic, handwritten scrawl introduced as "Justice for John & Yoko!" that included a healthy dose of cynicism:

> *John and Yoko add a great voice and drive to this country's so-called ART INSTITUTION / They inspire and transcend and stimulate that by doing so, only they can help others to see pure light and in doing that put an end to this wild dull taste of petty commercialism which is being passed off as artist art by the overpowering mass media. Hooray for John & Yoko! Let them stay and live here and breathe. The country's got plenty of room and space.*

.   .   .

THE NAMES JERRY Rubin, Abbie Hoffman, and Rennie Davis
were notably absent from the defense side of the showdown
between the INS and John Lennon. The New Left and Yippie
leaders—those who had enlisted Lennon to play the concert that
kick-started the deportation effort—didn't rally to the cause.
Curiously, there was also a void in support from the antiestablishment rebels of rock and roll. *Rolling Stone* writer Ralph J.
Gleason wondered, "Where the hell is everybody?" The very
musicians whom Lennon inspired were sadly silent. Had the
generation become as apathetic as Lennon hinted in Ann Arbor?

"There was no effort by Jerry or anyone to make the John Lennon immigration issue a Movement issue," Jay Craven says.

On the other hand, support from suspected criminals—including those with active suspended sentences—might have been more
trouble than help, something Lennon seemed to realize by then.
Recording work and trips to Texas demanded much of his time, and
he hadn't formally committed to Rubin's uncertain plans. The antic-
ipated tour leading up to an August finale was an idea that faded
into memory. And perhaps the absence of letters of support from
people in the Movement was judicious, came from their recognition
that their letters might hurt rather than help Lennon's case.

"Things just went on hiatus then moved, before long, to backing off," Craven says. "For all intents and purposes, that was it.
There was not going to be anything further."

The assumption by some was that Lennon felt conflicted
because of the pressures of deportation, and perhaps didn't want

to rock that particular boat. Rennie Davis says he was disappointed, but understood.

"The Justice Department came down on John with all fours," Davis says. "When John Sinclair was released, John [Lennon] was basically threatened with deportation. I have no criticism for John and Yoko for what they did. They stood tall and fought their fight. But the long and short of it was, John withdrew from the plan to go to the convention."

Going on tour was something Lennon had wanted to do for months, regardless of the political motivation. He liked the idea of a concert being one element of a larger rally for the benefit of New Left ideas, but he also knew what he didn't want.

"I don't want to create a riot or a fight in each town," Lennon said. "I just really want to paint it red."[11]

Rubin may have made one too many cryptic, by-any-means-necessary comments for Lennon's taste by then, which is not to say that there was any softening of his political views. Leni Sinclair says that the decision to distance himself from Rubin was singular.

"He felt they mislead him and he was not really in agreement with their tactics," Leni says. "So he disassociated himself from them."

Lennon told his friend, photographer Bob Gruen, that he wanted no part of Rubin's disruption-based protests. "John made it clear that he was not in total agreement with his revolutionary friends," Gruen wrote years later. "In everyday conversations he stuck to his view that the only way to change the system was to do so nonviolently." Lennon was clear in his convictions of promoting peace, but told Gruen it wasn't an Englishman's place to openly support a candidate or partisan platform.

Although Lennon decided not to join Rubin's anticampaign, he continued voicing his opinions publicly with appearances that included a rainy April 22 antiwar rally in New York's Bryant Park, a date sandwiched between INS hearing appointments. Lennon told the crowd he remained committed to a campaign for peace.

"I've heard the Movement is over—ha-ha!" Lennon mocked.[12] It wasn't over: he was still there, on full display as seen in the next day's newspapers, joined by demonstrators who had a personal stake in the game, Vietnam Veterans Against the War.

Among the leaders of that group was a recently returned soldier whose combat decorations included three Purple Hearts, a Bronze Star, and a Silver Star. A few weeks prior to the Bryant Park event, Massachusetts activist John Kerry had fronted an Operation POW march to Boston and joined a "ragtag crowd of veterans" who sang "Give Peace a Chance." Kerry was invited to introduce Lennon in New York, as related in Douglas Brinkley's biography, *Tour of Duty*:

> *"Lennon had seen my Senate Foreign Relations Committee speech on TV," Kerry recalled. "He liked what I was saying. Our government was giving him some flak because of his antiwar statements. So he asked me to be the guy to introduce him at the New York event. I met him ahead of time. We just hung around and talked."[13]*

The moment was captured in a photograph of the bomber-jacket-wearing Kerry side by side with Lennon; four decades later, that image hung with pride in Kerry's United States Senate office. "I love the picture because I love John Lennon," said Kerry, who transferred his office in 2013 to that of secretary of state.

Lennon stood proud at public rallies, gladly taking stage or raising a fist in support of the cause, well aware that those images would make the newspapers—and surveillance reports. Everything Lennon did was subject to scrutiny, some of which was comically misdirected. In April Apple issued a Lennon-produced LP by David Peel and the Lower East Side Band, *The Pope Smokes Dope*; Peel's pro-pot position was attributed to the album's producer in federal reports. One FBI source asked of Lennon: "Didn't he say something about the pope should smoke grass?"[14]

Lennon's music had long been misunderstood by some, especially those with a hidden agenda. As reported in *Rolling Stone*, investigators considered the merits of using the man's music against him as a legal strategy for deportation. The idea was to bring a stereo into court and play "Lennon albums [and] songs supporting such subversions as Irish freedom, women's lib, the rights of blacks and Indians, the decriminalization of marijuana."

According to the FBI, feminism and civil rights for blacks and Native Americans qualified as "subversions."

•　　•　　•

RATHER THAN KEEP quiet and go away, John and Yoko stood strong from a nondescript brownstone in Greenwich Village. Justice appeared to be on their side, or at least willing to give them some time.

On May 2, Judge Bernard J. Lasker signed a temporary restraining order that blocked the INS from holding a scheduled deportation hearing.[15] Wildes would be given adequate time to file motions, which would be heard by the court before anyone was ordered out of the country. Typical of court dockets everywhere, it would be a while before the parties went back before a judge.

Distancing Lennon from US shores would not be as simple as the administration initially thought. The INS ruled that John and Yoko were "outstanding artists," a declaration that—coupled with Yoko's custody order—could offset the marijuana charge and pave the way to permanent residence.

The *New York Times* explained the case in an editorial, "Love It and Leave It," and observed the irony of a government agency attempting to remove an unabashed cheerleader for a city and country.[16] True, Lennon rubbed some people the wrong way. The *Times* quoted a former Liverpool headmaster who told a tale of having to "cane" the fifth-grade future Beatle. He forgot the crime for which corporal punishment was dealt, but recalled Lennon as being "a thorough nuisance."

Perhaps, the *Times* suggested, in some people's minds Lennon was the same "nuisance" as he'd been as a child. Others disagreed passionately, but it didn't matter—the government was grossly overstepping its bounds and trampling on the First Amendment by penalizing a man for his opinions. The *Times* echoed the volume of letters that said forcing a separation of family was nothing less than cruelty, absent any sense of justice: "It would be ironic if the guardians of this country's private morals and public safety were to become known as the authors of a new slogan: 'America—Love It and Leave It.' What the Beatles might have done with such a refrain!"

Leon Wildes was justifiably encouraged by the temporary

injunction, yet concerned that there was more to the story. Wildes was surprised at the level of importance given the case. INS district director Sol Marks was among those Wildes felt was taking a too-active interest in the matter.

"When the immigration judge rendered his decision, he held a press conference," Wildes says. "He'd been saying that nothing could be done for Lennon, and he had an obligation as district director to remove or deport every illegal alien. That wasn't so."

Wildes encountered opposition that he hadn't seen in his considerable experience with INS proceedings. A technical error—the name of a federal agency used as a reference for Lennon—created a minor yet telling disturbance.

"The Lennons worked with the American Bar Association, which had a drug function to encourage young people to get off drugs and so on," Wildes says. During his arguments Wildes mistakenly referred to the ABA's efforts as being part of Nixon's antidrug organization. An honest mistake, corrected in later briefs, but the scope of the response told Wildes there was more to the fight than he first thought.

"The FBI went into a tizzy," Wildes says. "They investigated it with four different officers. It didn't take much to mislead them." Wildes watched in amazement as amateur mistakes piled up and revealed a sense of desperation, an unusual amount of effort to deport two relatively harmless individuals.

"The director, J. Edgar himself, was on the job and wrote some of the memos," Wildes said. "They were breathing down our necks, Lennon's and mine. They were getting nastier all the time . . . we were fighting for our lives there."

CHAPTER 5

WORDPLAY

*"John and Yoko . . . face
deportation. Deportation is
usually reserved for high-
ranking Mafia officials."*
—DICK CAVETT

ON MAY 2, 1972, the day of the restraining order that allowed John
and Yoko to remain in the US for the time being, J. Edgar Hoover died.

The impact of Hoover's death far exceeded the usual disrup-
tions caused by the sudden loss of an agency's top man; the position Hoover had created for himself over half a century inflated
the job to one whose power was surpassed only by the office of
the president; some questioned at times who truly held more.

Hoover first chaired a department named the Bureau of Investigation in 1924; in 1935 became first-ever director of what had

been rechristened the Federal Bureau of Investigation. Through Prohibition, World War II, the McCarthy fifties, and the civil rights era, Hoover held unprecedented authority in Washington, power that grew with each commander in chief he served.

Hoover's many critics said he interpreted his job as heading the "Bureau of Intimidation" for his legacy of harassment of Communists, subversive elements, homosexuals, dissenting voices, and anyone else he thought unpatriotic. When conventional information-gathering tactics weren't enough he created additional resources and authority: it wasn't until 1971 that the American public learned of Cointelpro, Hoover's counterintelligence program launched in 1956 to seek out dissenting political opinions, what many would call unwarranted spying. Targets in Hoover's crosshairs ranged from Charlie Chaplin to Martin Luther King Jr. to John Lennon; the former Beatle was one of Hoover's final projects.

To succeed Hoover, Nixon appointed L. Patrick Gray as the bureau's acting director. A retired Navy captain turned lawyer, Gray served as a congressional liaison with the Pentagon before he accepted a 1970 Department of Justice appointment. The acting director assumed ownership of Hoover's many streams of correspondence, although Associate Director Mark Felt supervised day-to-day Bureau operations.

Among Hoover's final memos were those involving John Lennon. Day one for Gray included a May 3 update on Lennon's deportation. Any hopes Hoover might have had for a low-key, discreet investigation and forced departure were long gone. Gray inherited a very public battle that would be played out in the newspapers and on national television.

•   •   •

"JOHN AND YOKO were here once before," Dick Cavett introduced his guests. "They face deportation. Deportation is usually reserved for high-ranking Mafia officials."[1]

So began a May 11, 1972, appearance by the Lennons on the *Dick Cavett Show*, a late-night talkfest helmed by the Nebraska-born writer-comedian. Through the '60s Cavett had written jokes for Jack Paar, served as a game-show panelist, and hosted a morning chat show before taking a late-night slot opposite Johnny Carson's *Tonight Show*. Cavett's intellectual inclinations made finding his place on network TV a challenge.

That his guests might be controversial was by design rather than accident; Cavett pursued and welcomed on-air talk more substantial than plugging a new movie, song, or TV show, including a notable June 1971 debate on Vietnam; arguments for US withdrawal by Veterans Against the War leader John Kerry clearly outscored a "we will win" approach. Cavett recalled the backlash in *Talk Show*, including President Nixon reportedly asking, "Is there any way we can screw [Cavett]? There must be ways."

Well regarded among rock's elite—visitors to his stage had included Jimi Hendrix, Janis Joplin, and a fresh-from-Woodstock Stephen Stills—Cavett had eagerly accepted an invitation in the summer of 1971 to meet with John and Yoko in their temporary St. Regis hotel quarters. They struck a show business quid pro quo: Cavett gamely appeared in one of the many short films made by the Lennons; John and Yoko agreed to guest on Cavett's show and did so for the first time in September 1971.

The episode was all talk, no tunes—a free-flowing conversation that took more than the allotted airtime and was broadcast over two nights. Cavett wasn't about to cut short reflections on a decade by a Beatle; they had been, he said, "the most written about, most listened to and most imitated musical group of the '60s . . . unequaled in affecting a decade of what young people looked like and thought about."

That was then, Lennon said. He enjoyed the ride and was proud of the work, but was now ready for life as an adult, not a teen idol: "When you grow up, we don't want to be dragged on stage playing 'She Loves You' when you've got asthma and tuberculosis when we're fifty. I said I didn't want to be singing 'She Loves You' when I'm thirty; I said that when I was twenty-five which in a roundabout way meant I wouldn't be doing whatever I was doing then at thirty."

As he said in January 1971 when interviewed by *Red Mole* and *Rolling Stone*, Lennon again pledged his commitment to the Movement on the Cavett show, discussing the roles of youth protest and civil disobedience.

"I don't believe in violent revolution, which is playing the same establishment games," Lennon clarified. "We're revolutionary artists, not gunmen. I'm still for peace, but I'm an artist first, politician second."

Lennon pointed out that even among supporters of the same cause there were disagreements as to how the goals could be achieved. Equally puzzling was how people who supported pacifist ideals had such disparate ideas about how to stage a proper protest; at the time he had yet to meet David Peel, the Elephants, and Jerry Rubin.

"A lot of people say, 'We don't want you to demonstrate for peace that way; we want you to do it our way,'" Lennon reflected. Eight months later in 1972, Lennon would have another Cavett-hosted conversation, ready to talk about getting involved, life under federal surveillance, and the definition of a controversial word in his new song.

• • •

BEFORE HE EVEN took his seat upon returning to Dick Cavett's stage in May 1972, John Lennon unknowingly violated a television taboo.

He didn't realize his somewhat minor mistake, a by-product of his flawed eyesight. Network rules held that guests on the show were not allowed to endorse a political candidate by name. Prior to Lennon's segment the first half of the program featured actress Shirley MacLaine, who was campaigning that year on behalf of a Democratic presidential hopeful. Equal-time considerations prevented MacLaine from specifically naming her candidate of choice.

Lennon was introduced, strolling onstage with a wave to the audience before shaking hands with Cavett and MacLaine. He noticed a small campaign button she wore, and leaned toward her for a closer look.

"What's his name?" Lennon asked, squinting at the badge. "Oh, 'McGovern.' I thought it said 'McCartney.' Bad eyes, you know."

Thus was solved the not-much-of-a-mystery as to which candidate MacLaine had been talking about for the past half-hour.

"You can say it," MacLaine laughed. "You're leaving anyway."

That, too, was probably something the network executives would have preferred not to be discussed on a talk show; government policy and court cases were best left to the news programs. Cavett, however, encouraged such debate. MacLaine had shared her experiences on the campaign trail, how people across the country were smarter than some wanted to believe. "They want to be told the truth," MacLaine said. "People think corruption is synonymous with leadership, and that an honest person can't govern."

Cavett was up-front with his interest in Lennon, and had previewed his guests' status during the show's opening: "Not only is it interesting to see them perform, but they're involved in a crucial court case to determine whether they can remain in the country or face deportation."

Lennon's life had for some time been an open book that he freely shared. The FBI wondered about his drug use, but he and the other Beatles had acknowledged their experiments, and each in time their reasons for putting drugs in the past. Whether or not that made them role models was another question entirely: "I never felt any responsibility, being a so-called idol," Lennon said after McCartney had admitted to trying LSD. "It's wrong of people to expect it. What they are doing is putting their responsibilities on us. They should have been responsible enough and not printed it if they were genuinely worried about people copying [us]."

Lennon had been honest—bluntly so at times—on most every aspect of his life; spiritual matters, fame, his partnership with the Beatles, and relationship with Yoko had all factored in his art and interviews. He was news, and the INS hearings and search for Kyoko were public knowledge.

The deportation effort was fueled by politics, he said, and the tragedy was that the government's desired result would split up a family.

"There was no arrangement made for the child," Lennon said of the agreement between Anthony Cox and Yoko. Disregarding the evident motivations of Cox trying to capitalize on his ex-wife's new wealth, Lennon made it seem as if the conflict was just like the battles fought in any divorce: "You know how those things get, and they got worse and worse until it came that we couldn't see Kyoko anymore."

Lennon broke the "fourth wall" between viewer and performer. He stared at the camera and spoke directly to Cox . . . and the INS: "We're saying it now if you're watching—we couldn't hide her anywhere. Yoko always said she thinks the child should be able to see both parents, have the benefit of both parents. Immigration's policy has always been not to split a family: Let us stay here because her daughter's here."

Ever conscious of public and government perceptions, Lennon clarified the reputation of his attorney, Leon Wildes. "He's not a radical," Lennon said. Wildes was a seasoned immigration specialist and not a civil rights activist like Chicago Seven counsel William Kunstler.

"It's very ironic that the government approved our application as outstanding artists whose presence is beneficial to US cultural interests and welfare," Lennon said. His attorney had been quite surprised by the maneuverings. "It's the only time he's had to go to court to force the government to consider an application like that."

Cavett read highlights from the letters of support received by
the INS from diverse sources that included United Auto Workers
boss Leonard Woodcock. MacLaine added her agreement, telling
Lennon: "You're more responsible for the expression of love and
peace in the arts than anyone practically in the twentieth century."

As Lennon told anyone who asked, he believed that his deportation was based on political motivations and not a marijuana
conviction. His opinions hadn't changed from "All You Need Is
Love" through "Give Peace a Chance." What was different, he
said, was who his friends in New York were. The assumption of
guilt by association made Lennon bridle and he hastened to set
the record straight: "We want peace; we said the same thing for
two years. [But] we're getting blamed for the Chicago convention
now. They think we're going to San Diego or Miami or wherever
it is. We ain't going. There will be no big jam with us and Dylan,
there's too much going on."

That statement was not reported by the FBI agents in the
audience. Instead, a memo cited Lennon's passing reference
to a gathering at the Washington Square Methodist Church, a
small benefit concert where Elephant's Memory was slated to
perform: "After Lennon plugged it on the Dick Cavett Show, the
benefit concert for the Attica Defense Committee turned a larger
crowd than expected." The event "netted $2,000 for the Defense
Command [and] $200 for the WSM Church." Even by early 1970s
economic standards, hardly a sum worth the trouble to report.[2]

•   •   •

WHAT SCARED THE network most was the song title's single, six-letter word: "Nigger." Would John Lennon get away with breaking existing broadcast standards?

"I remember talking about it with my wife before we went over to the studio," Gary Van Scyoc says. "I wasn't sure it was going to fly, and John might change his mind at the last minute and do something else. But he didn't."

The song itself took about five minutes to perform; preliminary discussion of the lyrics took much longer.

"When that song hit, it was like a bomb going off, it was a mess," Van Scyoc says. "John didn't understand what all the fuss was about. He was kind of naïve, I guess, as were we all. He just didn't think it was going to get that kind of reaction."

Cavett knew the response it would get: the FCC was very clear on certain things. Lennon couldn't expect to perform, for instance, "Working Class Hero" on TV, not with the word "fuck" in the lyrics. Even the allegedly progressive FM stations hesitated to send the f-bomb through their transmitters; record store owners wondered if the printed lyrics on album covers violated obscenity laws. *Rolling Stone* editor Ben Fong-Torres had addressed the prevailing attitudes: "Stations around the country say they want to play 'Working Class Hero' . . . But, with very few exceptions, they're all too fucking scared."[3]

What they were scared of was unclear: penalties were little more than a slap on the wrist, and that was only if someone actually complained. FCC broadcast analyst June Herrick did not recall any specific backlash about "Working Class Hero," or even Jefferson Airplane's "up against the wall, motherfuckers" when

142 THE WALRUS AND THE ELEPHANTS

PBS aired a San Francisco concert performance. The bigger challenge was identifying which lyrics advocated drug use through the use of ever-changing slang terms. Herrick said that about 1,500 letters a month made claims about "drug songs," most of which were red-herring alarms such as "Lucy in the Sky with Diamonds" and claims that the "LSD" acronym was intentional. Lennon had said he was surprised at the discovery and started checking through old lyrics just to be sure. (When the Beatles wanted to sing about drug use, they did: code-breaking skills were not needed to decipher "I get high with a little help from my friends.")

In the early 1970s language and drug references took a backseat to other broadcast issues. Federal monitors, said program manager Larry Lee of KPFT-FM in Houston, "were more worried about the political content" of rock songs such as Neil Young's "Ohio," which took a decidedly antipresidential stance.

"Woman Is the Nigger of the World" presented so many questions in so short a phrase. Lennon had insisted the song be issued as the first single from Some Time in New York City—against many opposing opinions at Apple—and was equally determined to sing it on the Dick Cavett Show. Lennon wanted people to hear the song, and one method was secured when Apple advertised a telephone number that people could call and listen to the single, a 1972 version of on-demand media.

The performance was approved on condition that the host read a disclaimer, a previously recorded and approved statement that was inserted into the broadcast. Cavett's discomfort and distaste was obvious as he read the statement:

> *John and Yoko got into something which ABC feels*
> *may develop into, in their words, a highly contro-*
> *versial issue. It revolves around the song, "Woman*
> *Is the Nigger of the World," and the obvious fact*
> *that some members of our black audience will or*
> *may be offended by the use of that word. In the next*
> *segment, John Lennon gives his reason for writing*
> *the song and for using the word. I permitted this*
> *insertion into the show as the only alternative to a*
> *full deletion by ABC of the full segment.*[4]

"This is a song about the women's problem," Lennon said. "Obviously there were a few people who reacted strangely to it, but usually they were white and male."

The song's title was credited to Yoko, who used the phrase during an interview she had given two years earlier to an English women's magazine. The poetic nature of the comparison struck a note with Lennon, not unlike occasions when Ringo Starr came up with phrases such as "hard day's night" or "tomorrow never knows" and unknowingly gave birth to Beatles songs. Yoko's input was more than just a song title, and he'd frequently acknowledged her awakening—often through artistic means— his own guilt in how he regarded women.

"I was more of a chauvinist than I am now," Lennon said. "Like everybody else I talked more and more about it in the last two years. It became more of a thing and I had to find out about it myself."

The feminist movement may have been the song's driving force, but Lennon said the word choice prompted a separate battle: "A lot of stations were saying we're not going to play this because it says nigger and a white man shouldn't say it."

To support the use of the word as metaphor Lennon read aloud a "definition" as penned by Representative Ron Dellums from California, a founding member of the Congressional Black Caucus. The definition had been included in promotional materials for the single, including an Apple Records ad in *Billboard* magazine. "This great guy came out with this, which is fantastic," Lennon explained before reading Dellums's proclamation: "If you define niggers as someone whose lifestyle is defined by others, whose opportunities are defined by others, whose role in society is defined by others, then good news!—You don't have to be black to be a nigger in this society. Most of the people in America are niggers."

Lennon finished, and seemed surprised by the spirited applause that followed. He laughed and reminded people he was just a musical journalist; please don't deport the messenger: "Oh my goodness: we'll never get in now."

In spite of ABC's misgivings, Cavett invited "you two menaces to society" to perform, and John and Yoko took the stage with Elephant's Memory.

Lennon plugged his guitar into an amp, strummed a chord, adjusted the volume. He turned to his band, kicked the stage four times, counted out loud for another measure. A thump from drummer Rick Frank, wailing saxophone from Stan Bronstein. Lennon belted out the opening lyrics, blues-ballad style: "Woman is the nigger of the world . . . yes she is: think about it."

The band enjoyed brief spotlights: Bronstein's solo ended one

Welcome to America: John Lennon and Yoko Ono with their friend, the host of *The Dick Cavett Show*, in September 1971. (Ann Limongello, Getty Images.)

Backstage at *The Dick Cavett Show* in September 1971. John considers a wardrobe choice while Cavett chats with Yoko. (Getty Images.)

(*Right*) John and Yoko perform at the December 1971 John Sinclair Freedom Rally in Ann Arbor's Crisler Arena, backed by musicians from David Peel's Lower East Side. (Getty Images.)

FREE JOHN SINCLAIR AND ALL POLITICAL PRISONERS!

JOHN SINCLAIR FREEDOM RALLY

NATION

NATION

FRIDAY DEC 10 1971

FRIDAY DEC 10 1971

JOHN LENNON & YOKO ONO
STEVIE WONDER · BOB SEGER · COMMANDER CODY
ED SANDERS · BOBBY SEALE · TEAGARDEN & VANWINKLE · ALLEN GINSBERG
PHIL OCHS · ARCHIE SHEPP & ROSWELL RUDD WITH CJQ · JERRY RUBIN · THE UP
RENNIE DAVIS · DAVE DELLINGER · DAVID PEEL · FR. JAMES GROPPI
MC's BOB RUDNICK & ANNE LAVASSEUR

CRISLER ARENA
ANN ARBOR

©1993 GARY GRIMSHAW

A commemorative poster was reprinted after the John Sinclair Freedom Rally concert at Ann Arbor's Crisler Arena. The names of surprise guests Stevie Wonder and hometown hero Bob Seger did not appear on the original 1971 poster.

(*Left*) New Left leader Rennie Davis joined John and Yoko at an informal February 1972 courthouse press conference responding to deportation orders. (Leni Sinclair.)

John counseled guitarist Wayne "Tex" Gabriel (left), while keyboardist Adam Ippolito stood ready at the Record Plant for early 1972 sessions for *Some Time in New York City*. (Mike Jahn.)

(*Left*) John and the Elephants at the Record Plant while recording *Some Time in New York City*, 1972. (Mike Jahn.)

Rock royalty entertained the *Mike Douglas Show* audience in February 1972 as John and Yoko share stage time with Chuck Berry, a band that included Elephant's Memory founder Stan Bronstein (left), and Yippie leader Jerry Rubin on bongos. (Corbis.)

(*Left*) Bassist Gary Van Scyoc jams with John at the Record Plant while recording *Some Time in New York City*, 1972. (Mike Jahn.)

(*Next page, left*) Bandsmen noted the bond formed between John and guitarist Wayne "Tex" Gabriel, who spent "hours sitting cross-legged on the floor" during studio sessions. (Bob Gruen.)

(*Next page, right*) John's presence in New York attracted many famous guests to the studio, including an impromptu jam with Mick Jagger and Wayne "Tex" Gabriel. (Bob Gruen.)

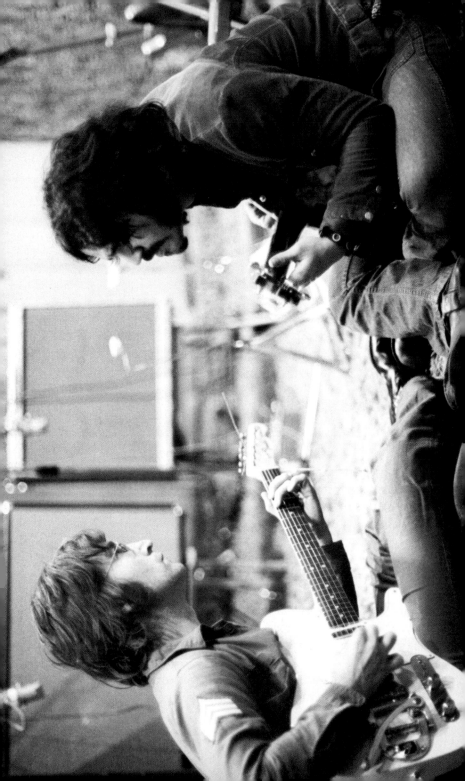

(*Left and above*) John and Yoko rallied the masses during a February 1972 protest in front of the British Overseas Airways office in New York. The protest called for withdrawal of British troops from Ireland in the wake of the "Bloody Sunday" riots. (AP Photo/Ron Frehm.)

Yoko flashing a peaceful wish while John answered reporters' questions after a May 1972 Immigration and Naturalization Services hearing. (Corbis.)

(*Right*) Lennon's "new band" as featured on the *Some Time in New York City* album in June 1972. From left: Gary Van Scyoc, John, Yoko, Wayne "Tex" Gabriel, Rick Frank, Adam Ippolito, and Stan Bronstein. (Bob Gruen.)

(*Next page*) Gary Van Scyoc, Wayne "Tex" Gabriel, and Rick Frank keep pace with Lennon during August rehearsals for the One-to-One concert. (Bob Gruen.)

One-to-One: John peforms "Mother" at Madison Square Garden in August 1972. (Corbis.)

(*Previous page*) The May 1972 *Dick Cavett Show* appearance by John, Yoko, and Elephant's Memory drew considerable attention from the network over the performance of "Woman is the Nigger of the World." (Bob Gruen.)

(*Right*) Yoko takes a vocal turn at Madison Square Garden, backed by John and the Elephants. (Bob Gruen.)

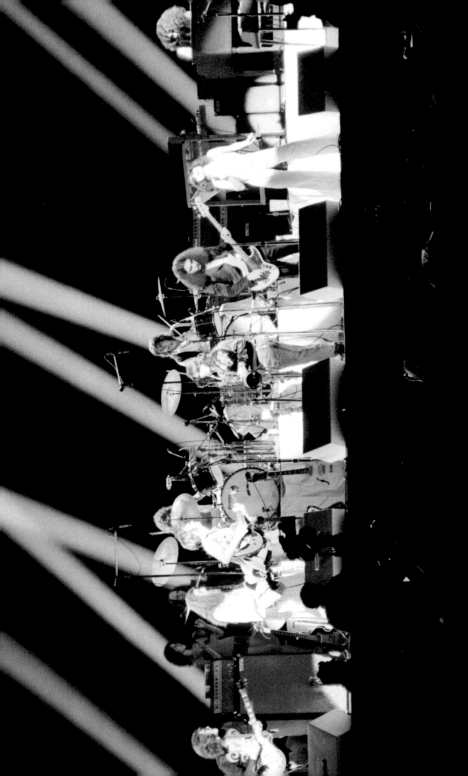

Attorney Leon Wildes with John and Yoko in April 1973 for the declaration of "Nutopia," of which the Lennons were ambassadors seeking diplomatic immunity. (Corbis.)

A short-haired John with Yoko during the Watergate hearings in June 1973. The Lennons were invited to watch the proceedings by Democratic Senator Sam Ervin. (Corbis.)

Famous faces seen at the Record Plant included ballet master Rudolf Nureyev and reporter-friend Geraldo Rivera, who spearheaded the One-to-One concert at Madison Square Garden. (Bob Gruen.)

(*Left*) Ready for a show: For Lennon's first—and only—full-length solo concert in August 1972, additional musicians joined the Plastic Ono Elephant's Memory Band lineup to better fill the Madison Square Garden arena. From left: bassists John Ward and Gary Van Scyoc, Wayne "Tex" Gabriel, drummers Jim Keltner and Rick Frank, Adam Ippolito, and Stan Bronstein, along with *Some Time in New York City* album producer Phil Spector, reclining before John and Yoko. (Bob Gruen.)

(*Next page*) John displays his long-sought green card, issued in July 1976. (Bob Gruen.)

verse, Gabriel's guitar pierced with equal rage after another.

"We insult her every day on TV," Lennon sang.

The song faded to end. John unplugged his guitar and he and Yoko walked down two steps to rejoin Cavett while the band rang out the final notes.

The response, of course, was not what the corporate suits feared.

"As I predicted, there was a great deal of protest—about the mealy mouth apology," Cavett recalled years later. "I don't think there were any about the song."[5]

•   •   •

RON DELLUMS WAS well aware that his definition wasn't normally discussed on national television, let alone by a Beatle.

"I had no idea that a guy like John Lennon would use the term to write a major song," Dellums says. "'Woman Is the Nigger of the World' is a very powerful idea."

Dellums proudly admits that his definition was influenced by the philosophy of Dr. Martin Luther King Jr. Ideology aside, he also knew that he was pushing people's buttons by defining the word as he did.

"My interest in writing it was not to be cute," Dellums says. "It was an effort to make a very serious point to the African American community and to the broader community: that we need to mobilize based on our mutual and enlightened self-interest. Many of us in society are being oppressed, and if we come together we can throw off the yoke of oppression."

Born in 1935 in Oakland, Dellums had served in the US Marine
Corps during the early days of troop integration in the 1950s
before graduating from the University of California, Berkeley,
with the help of the GI bill and whatever part-time jobs he could
get. (He had been denied a scholarship after high school; in
response he joined the Marines.) He began work both as a psy-
chiatric social worker and campus-based political activist before
his 1967 election to the Berkeley City Council. That two-year
term led to his election to national office, and Dellums joined
the US House as a congressman in 1970, a seat he would hold for
nearly thirty years. In 1972 Dellums cofounded the Congressional Black Caucus, which consisted of thirteen members of the
House and Senate. Women were equally underrepresented, and
accounted for just fifteen seats in that Ninety-Second Congress.

Dellums's point—and Lennon's in his lyrics—was that 1972
America was very much a white man's world. Change—as
always—starts from within and is rarely won alone. The feminist
movement required a redefinition for men as well as women; the
civil rights movement needed more than just black leadership.

"Martin Luther King did not die solely for the liberation of
black people," Dellums says. "Martin Luther King died trying to
evolve an egalitarian society. The civil rights movement in many
ways was the inspiration for every other movement that emerged
in the sixties."

Dellums says the motivation behind his attempt to redefine
a word was an effort to change how people heard it: "The term
nigger has been used historically as a derogatory term referring
to black people. I decided that somebody black ought to redefine

nigger and look at it from a different perspective. Number two was to help people understand the need for coalition politics: we alone—meaning black people—could not change the world."

But a shared consciousness might be the first step, and the civil rights movement gave birth to movements on behalf of individual liberties and other minority rights movements—Latino rights and gay rights, environmental activism, and consumer advocacy.

"A group of people in this country stood up and said, 'That's it, I've had enough, and we've got to move toward a just society. We can organize the niggers and change America and change the world,'" Dellums says. "If you're uncomfortable with the term 'nigger,' then insert the term 'oppressed,' it's the same point."

Dellums says that carving a wide philosophical path—with admitted shock value to gain attention—was a risky approach. Those taking that avenue could be easily dismissed; few could successfully put it out to a large audience.

"In walks John Lennon and Yoko," Dellums says. "Here were people who used their authenticity, their celebrity, and attention to raise issues in different ways. I appreciated and respected that because it was in the aggregate that all of us made our own little contributions that, in the whole scheme of things, added up to significant change."

•   •   •

AS ONE OF the final obsessions of J. Edgar Hoover, the quest to oust John Lennon made a suitable bookend to the FBI director's career; the case was eerily similar to that of another artist who was both popular and political. In the early 1920s Assistant Director Hoover had made note of Charlie Chaplin's alliances with allegedly dissident minds, and considered the actor a "parlor Bolsheviki." By the McCarthy era, Hoover had listed the Britain-born Chaplin as a likely Communist, and when Chaplin flew to London for the 1952 premiere of *Limelight*, Hoover had the INS revoke the actor's reentry visa. Chaplin remained exiled from America until 1972, when he was given an honorary Oscar award.

The similarities with John Lennon's immigration status did not go unnoticed by the media. "Shades of the Charlie Chaplin fiasco," the *New York Times* noted, "for which the country has just got through apologizing."[6] Elsewhere, an ever-broader circle of supporters rallied to Lennon's defense. Metropolitan Museum director Thomas Hoving told the *New York Times* in May that if Lennon "were a painting he would be hanging in the Metropolitan Museum, benevolently on the wall." The Episcopal bishop of New York, the Right Reverend Paul Moore Jr., said he'd gotten to know the Lennons and that he would "welcome and delight in their presence in New York."[7]

INS hearings in May featured in-person testimony on Lennon's behalf, including an appearance by Dick Cavett. In his book *Talk Show*, Cavett describes not only his courtroom time but, viewed in proper perspective, the odds against Lennon remaining in America.[8] Cavett recalls an unsettling segment of the infamous Oval Office recordings: "On one of the Nixon tapes, the president's henchman and lickspittle H. R. Haldeman can be heard educating his boss—who was minimally knowledgeable of popular culture—about Lennon's vast popularity, with the words 'This guy could sway an election.'"[9]

Having found himself under suspicion from Washington after the Vietnam debate, Cavett was aware of the potential risk in supporting a federal target. Not long after Lennon's appearances on his show, the IRS audited Cavett's entire staff. Other similar reports would be heard of Nixon "illegally wielding the IRS as a weapon—sometimes ruining lives," Cavett said.

Being under constant watch, subject to telephone wiretaps, and often followed by federal agents became just another fact of life for Lennon and his associates, including the members of Elephant's Memory.

"I used to see them in my building all the time," Van Scyoc says. "It was something going on in the underbelly, but nobody was letting it get in the way of learning the next song or doing our jobs as a backup band and making John happy."

Given their own history with Jerry Rubin and other radical souls, they accepted a certain amount of police scrutiny. The intensity of the interest in Lennon, however, was a bit jarring.

"We talked about maybe there being a file on each of us," Ippolito says. "But that was pretty much it. Hoover and Nixon were trying to get him out of the country. Nixon, being the maniac that he was, you could imagine what went through his brain when he thought John Lennon would get the vote out for Democrats."

•   •   •

"I DON'T KNOW if there's any mercy to plead for because this isn't a Federal Court," Lennon said to Judge Ira Fieldsteel when INS hearings concluded on May 17. "But if there is, I'd like it, please."[10]

The questions being raised—of forcing a woman to choose between husband and child, of singling out a distinguished artist for exile—had now become part of the national discourse. Was the government being unmerciful? Editorialists wondered why Lennon seemed to be the target of a personal vendetta. "Unhand that Beatle," demanded the *Washington Daily News*, noting that INS officials "must have better things to do" than deport John Lennon. There were more than a million illegal immigrants in America, "many of them taking jobs from citizens, committing crimes, or collecting welfare payments, and INS would do better to pursue them instead of Mr. Lennon."[11]

In late May Washington's National Press Club hosted a press conference organized by Ken Dewey—a member of the New York State Commission on Cultural Resources—on behalf of the National Committee for John and Yoko. Dewey issued a statement openly challenging the Nixon administration's use of executive authority: "If, as mounting evidence suggests, this couple is having difficulties simply because of their outspoken, sincere, and nonviolent opposition to the war in Vietnam and to related issues, then very serious questions about the misuse of governmental power must be raised."[12]

Speculation as to the government's motives ranged widely; *Rolling Stone* was close to the general truth: "selective" prosecution was at work. Fellow Beatle George Harrison similarly had a marijuana bust in his past, and not only spoke of peace but embraced foreign cultures and religions while doing so, yet freely traveled and worked in America. Canadian rocker Neil Young had—with partners Crosby, Stills & Nash—in 1970 recorded the Kent State response, "Ohio," which called the president out by name in its lyrics, but there's no evidence that the Nixon administration interfered with Young's travel plans.

Maybe it was a personal thing. Lennon was not always well liked by the Bible Belt crowd, and in simplistic terms it seemed to *Rolling Stone* that the government caved in to conservative pressure in the form of "letters and phone calls from a lot of old biddies."[13]

Within legal circles the hearings posed procedural and ethical questions that begged analysis. *New York Times* law columnist Grace Lichtenstein took note of the sometimes-tearful pleas when Yoko addressed the court. "You're asking me to choose between my child and my husband," Yoko said. "I don't think you can ask any human being to do that." Lichtenstein, like so many others, wondered why the government was trying so hard: "Even if they weren't John and Yoko, their case might warrant considerable attention as a challenge of American immigration laws."[14]

The effort to deport John Lennon had been put into a legal, bureaucratic machine that, if nothing else, could be a painfully slow process. The hearings ended inconclusively: Judge Fieldsteel gave Leon Wildes until July 1 to submit any additional motions or arguments. It was understood by veteran court watchers that, even if Fieldsteel ruled in favor of July deportation, Wildes would have the option to appeal and initiate another round of hearings. The *New York Times* explained, "Appeals could prolong this case for months, perhaps years. In which case the Lennons ironically would be forced to remain within the borders of the United States."

·   ·   ·

IF INVESTIGATORS WANTED to keep an eye on Lennon, the daily newspapers provided numerous clues as to his where-abouts and the types of "radical" associates that seemed to be on his side, meaning declared opponents of President Nixon. Lennon was seemingly unaware of the true political motivations against him—to block him from performing concerts to unseat a president—and was convinced that his pro-peace/antiwar state-ments were the root of his green card problems.

That belief didn't silence him. Two days after asking the court for mercy Lennon joined a May 19 vigil in Duffy Square, one of dozens held in major cities that day. The events were organized, according to the FBI, "by peace groups demanding complete withdrawal of US troops from Indochina."[15]

A growing number of rallies were supported by a broader and more influential demographic than the hippies: established names including Joseph Papp, Arthur Miller, and William Styron endorsed a group called the National Peace Action Coalition; membership included "local politicians and trade union leaders," as noted in full-page newspaper ads that announced the rally.

While Lennon hid in plain sight, cloak-and-dagger tactics continued but strategies to force a quicker deportation failed.

The combined resources of the FBI and NYPD couldn't put a joint in Lennon's hand—or at least the appearance of such to make a drug bust—as reported that month: "New York Police Department advised that his department has been unable to make a narcotics case on the Lennons. NYPD continuing." A separate plan was to prove that Yoko's claims of her ex-husband abducting Kyoko were false—allowing for a charge of perjury—and agents were sent to track down Tony Cox and the girl. That line of investigation quickly dissolved.

The acting director of the FBI seemed a more cautious fellow than the man he replaced. Without openly stating that any laws were broken—at least not on a piece of paper that might be viewed—Gray reminded agents on May 24 to be careful about bureau involvement in what were decidedly INS matters, whether tracking down Tony Cox and Kyoko or encouraging a drug arrest for Lennon.

"In view of possible court proceedings," Gray wrote, "active investigations by FBI could result in FBI Agents testifying which would not be in Bureau's best interest and could result in considerable adverse publicity."

Maybe it was the government's turn to succumb to paranoia. Suspicions ruled the day at the White House and throughout Washington in the summer of 1972. In spite of Lennon's televised assurance that he would not attend the August convention, some on Capitol Hill remained terrified of the prospect. On June 5 Gray advised the Miami office that Lennon was "planning a large rock concert in Miami during the convention, and that the rock concert was to be held in front of the convention hall."

What to do about Lennon was one of countless perceived problems to be put on the front burner by Nixon loyalists. A variety of sources—federal investigators, former CIA operatives, attorneys, and others—weren't going to tolerate any disruptive activities from the worst of the hippie radicals. One crew, said to include G. Gordon Liddy, pitched the aggressive plan of abducting certain protest leaders and dumping them in a Mexican desert for the duration. Stories were told by insiders including Jeb Magruder and John Ehrlichman of a proposal to snatch and stash Jerry Rubin and Abbie Hoffman; Attorney General John Mitchell successfully shot down unlawful imprisonment as a strategy.

But the John Lennon case would soon be of limited interest to the press, the public, or within the White House administration, the members of which had far greater priorities waiting for them. Rather than kidnap the hippies, Liddy and E. Howard Hunt directed a crew of burglars who made their way into the Democratic National Headquarters offices in the Watergate Hotel.

•　　•　　•

THE MEMBERS OF Elephant's Memory shared a unique rite of passage in John Lennon's career, that of a record being both a critical and commercial disappointment. *Some Time in New York City* proved to be everything that critics and the Nixon administration loved to hate. Released on June 12, the double-LP's cover alone was capable of annoying Lennon's Washington enemies: dominant on the newspaper-styled front page was a superimposed image of Richard Nixon dancing with Chairman Mao; both leaders appeared to be naked. Song titles were headlines, including prominent placement of "Woman Is the Nigger of the World." An assortment of puns, jokes, and gags included a small picture of producer Phil Spector, captioned, *To know him is to love him,* and a nod to the *New York Times'* slogan: *Ono News That's Fit to Print.*

The first of the double-album's discs featured the studio work of Lennon and the Elephants, ten songs including "John Sinclair," "Attica State," "Luck of the Irish," "Angela," and "New York City." The second disc—"Free Live Jam LP: John & Yoko and Star-Studded Cast of Thousands . . . yours at no extra cost"—was recorded at a June 1971 Fillmore East performance with Frank Zappa's Mothers of Invention, and a 1969 Plastic Ono Band show at London Lyceum. The tracks included Lennon's "Cold Turkey" and Yoko performing a long piece entitled "Don't Worry Kyoko."

Was it the politics that prevented the album from reaching commercial success, or was there too much Yoko and not enough Lennon? Or perhaps the topics were too specific—one man's marijuana woes, a black woman activist jailed by the man, British policies regarding Ireland—and Lennon's was not the only name on the credit lines. The album was the work of "John & Yoko / Plastic Ono Band with Elephant's Memory plus Invisible Strings"; the last being an inside joke referring to Spector's wall of sound. Unlike Lennon's previous post-Beatles albums, *Plastic Ono Band* and *Imagine,* on which he'd composed and performed the bulk of the material, *Some Time* afforded equal space to Yoko's work: Of the album's ten original songs only two—"New York City" and "John Sinclair"—were credited as Lennon compositions. Three songs were written by Yoko alone—"Sisters O Sisters," "We're All Water," and "Born in a Prison"; the rest had dual Lennon/Ono bylines.

The sale of 45s had taken a backseat to album-generated revenue by then, but hit songs still factored heavily in the commercial success of an LP. Lennon insisted on "Woman Is the Nigger of the World" as the lead single, a debut that challenged the album's commercial prospects.

Would the outcome have been different if another song had been chosen as the debut single? Gary Van Scyoc says that Lennon was doubly discouraged, both from the critical barbs and having "Woman Is the Nigger of the World" banned from mass-market play.

"There were a lot of positive things about it at the time," Van Scyoc says of the album, but the choice of its first single may have been too big an obstacle. "In the back of my mind I remember saying, 'Man, I don't know about this one.' But he was hell-bent on that one as the single. The bottom line is, as a record, when they banned it that was it. John was devastated; that was a new one on him."

Lennon had expected a certain amount of resistance to the album's political content. He also knew that the music press would be quick to pounce on Yoko Ono's vocal work, as she sang lead on several tracks. *Some Time* generated the harshest reviews Lennon had ever received, lyrically and musically. *Rolling Stone*'s Stephen Holden described an album that could kill a lesser career: "What can one say when confronted with incipient artistic suicide? Issue a warning and then try to accentuate the positive?"[16]

Holden did just that, and listed attributes including Lennon's "solid as ever" singing, and rare praise for the album's other vocalist: "Yoko's caterwauling yodel" was "worth a listen" on "We're All Water," Holden said. Also in the plus column was the playing of Elephant's Memory, "a terrific, hard-driving rock and roll band with a raunchy fifties sound . . . the strongest part of the album. Only Elephant's Memory emerges unscathed, [with] some taut, funky backups that are well suited to the Lennons' voices."

But the content of the songs met strong criticism: "Didactic political statements," in Holden's opinion, which did not properly address the issues at hand. As Lennon had previously observed, people wanted him to protest but also dictated the method and terms for doing so. "The tunes are shallow and derivative and the words little more than sloppy nursery rhymes that patronize the issues and individuals they seek to exalt," Holden lambasted.

The reviews were not unanimous, and some found elements to admire, particularly among New Yorkers. *Newsday*'s Robert Christgau argued that—quality of music aside—the album supported Lennon's bid for US residency:[17]

> *This new John Lennon album . . . proves conclusively that the ex-Beatle deserves to stay in America. My evidence is a line from a tune called "Attica State": "Come together join the Movement." No doubt the State Department, which persists in trying to deport him, thinks this makes Lennon a subversive, but I*

ask you, who but a true New Yorker would exhibit
such chutzpah?

Christgau wondered if Lennon's effort was worthwhile, and
echoed the sentiments expressed by Rennie Davis and others
that the revolution's golden years were now in the past: "Among
my Movement friends the line seems to be that there is no Movement," Christgau noted. "We want the world, but we'll settle for
George McGovern."

The reviewers wanted to like Lennon, to cheer the rebellious
voice so beloved by a generation, but a cynicism was developing that a generation's saviors weren't likely to come facto-
ry-wrapped on vinyl. According to Christgau, "Unless the music
business becomes a much stranger business than it already is,
the violent overthrow of the US government is not likely to come
in quadraphonic sound. It's no accomplishment to boogie ado-
lescents into youth rebellion any more. The hip young are rapidly
turning into another interest group, like labor unions."

Credit was given for Lennon taking risks, but Christgau was
among those who felt the album fell short of its lofty goals. The
songs were "more direct," which also meant they were "more
risky. They attack issues so simplistically that you wonder
whether the artists believe themselves. This time John appears
to have plunged too fast."

Leaning on the hybrid term for artistic agitation and pro-
paganda, Christgau cut to the chase: "Agitprop is one thing.
Wrong-headed agitprop is another. Agitprop that fails to reach
its constituency, however, is hardly a thing at all, and since

Lennon's forte has always been the communication of new truths to a mass audience, that possibility is very distressing. He isn't exploiting his charisma this time, he's gambling it."

Separate from the album itself, Christgau used the forum to criticize Lennon's brief adoption of Washington Square Park's favorite troubadour, and questioned if certain Village attitudes may have affected his art: "It's bad enough to praise David Peel and worse still to record him. But imitating his thoughtless hip-left orthodoxy is worst of all."

The bandsmen of Elephant's Memory said that the response—or reaction in some cases—weighed heavily on Lennon.

"The problem was, he was really still on his own as an ex-Beatle, and still had a lot to prove," Adam Ippolito says. "He still had the need to be successful; not financial but on a very basic and broad level."

In the United States the album *Some Time in New York City* peaked at forty-eight on Billboard's charts; the single "Woman Is the Nigger of the World" topped out at fifty-eight. A modest success for average musicians; a harsh disappointment for Lennon. Ippolito says the record's reviews and chart failure took a toll on John and Yoko, bringing to an end a period of artistic and political exploration.

"They went into hiding for at least a week when it came out," Ippolito says. The Elephants—and New Left leaders—had no idea what Lennon might do next.

CHAPTER 6

"WE'LL GET IT RIGHT NEXT TIME"

*"They were out to get him.
It can be very spooky to be
followed or wire tapped."*
—Paul Krassner

IF ANYONE NEEDED to get away, John Lennon and Yoko Ono were long overdue for a vacation in the summer of 1972. In San Francisco Lennon found a place similar to their now beloved Lower Manhattan. As with New York, Lennon wanted to believe he and Yoko could go about their business with little or no celebrity fanfare. They considered finding an apartment in San Francisco, a West Coast bookend to their Village loft. "We walked the streets all day, all over town and nobody hassled us," Lennon said.[1]

The underground newspaper publisher Paul Krassner met them

for lunch in late July. Krassner had been introduced to Yoko several
years earlier, and spent time with the Lennons in Syracuse at the
September 1971 opening of Yoko's Emerson Museum show. He was
a kindred spirit in many ways with Lennon. They shared a playful
sense of the absurd that was balanced and guided by compas-
sionate intelligence. In the early sixties Krassner had turned local
journalism into community activism; he interviewed a doctor who
performed abortions and followed up by establishing an underground referral service. Krassner indulged a theatrical side and tried
stand-up comedy after he edited Lenny Bruce's autobiography, *How
to Talk Dirty and Influence People*. Friends included some of the era's
most interesting and infamous, whether taking LSD with Groucho
Marx, romping as a Merry Prankster with Ken Kesey, launching the
Realist, or vying to unseat Nixon alongside Jerry Rubin and Rennie
Davis; Krassner was among the founders of the Youth International
Party and credited with coining the term Yippie.

By the summer of 1972, the antipresidential sentiment gained
momentum after the June break-in at the Democratic Party's
Watergate Hotel offices was discovered. Journalists across the
country tried to keep pace with Woodward and Bernstein as the
story unfolded, each new development raising questions as to just
how far up the ladder the scandal reached. There was talk of secret
White House accounts that financed the burglary, and the latest
revelations included the involvement of former Attorney General
John Mitchell, whose wife Martha had become a quotable media
darling. The flamboyant Mrs. Mitchell had been credited with
popularizing the presidential "Tricky Dick" nickname, and also
described Vietnam protestors as "Russian revolutionaries."

Martha had even juicier stories to tell in the wake of Watergate, and *Realist* reporter Mae Brussell explored a notable Beltway legend: "Why Was Martha Mitchell Kidnapped?" Mr. and Mrs. Mitchell were Watergate residents, and she claimed to have been forcibly silenced after the burglary. With Watergate, though, even the wildest theories often connected with actual targets.

Brussell's report joined a growing chorus of questions about Nixon and company. Each revelation heightened the sense of danger felt by those, like the Yippies, who were fighting the fight. Krassner thought that Lennon should know a few things about the White House he'd angered, an administration more than willing to co-opt the law on its own behalf. Krassner showed Lennon the printer's galleys of the Brussell article: the sheets awaited time on a printing press before the story went public.

Krassner had a story to tell, but as often was the case with independent publishers, he was short of the capital needed to get it in print. He told Lennon of his shortfall, and after lunch they went to a local bank to withdraw the $5,000 Krassner needed to get the presses rolling. Admittedly, Krassner showed the galleys to a man with a reputation for dropping cash to support efforts like the *Realist*.

Perhaps Lennon sympathized with a fellow suspect; he had a demonstrated soft spot for radicals known to be under federal watch, which Krassner surely was. Included in Krassner's FBI file—which he obtained years later under the Freedom of Information Act—was a letter sent to *Life* magazine in response to a favorable 1968 profile of Krassner and the *Realist*. Krassner, the author said, was not the lovable crusader portrayed by *Life*: "To classify Krassner as some sort of 'social rebel' is far too cute. He's a nut, a raving, unconfined nut. As for any intellectual rewards to be gleaned from *The Realist*—much better prose may be found on lavatory walls."[2]

The letter was signed, *Howard Rasmussen, Brooklyn College.* As recounted years later in the *Los Angeles Times*, "Rasmussen" was an FBI agent. Never failing to recognize a solid turn of phrase, Krassner entitled his autobiography *Confessions of a Raving Unconfined Nut.*

More grievously, while the Left included plenty of people who posed no real threat to the establishment—delusions of counterculture grandeur notwithstanding—that didn't matter to a corrupt government willing to abuse its authority to keep them quiet. Krassner says the Nixon-Beatle showdown resulted from a combination of factors—extreme abuse of presidential power and a cultural figure of rare if not unequaled stature.

Lennon confided to Krassner that he might have crossed a line, and perhaps some of his open defiance went too far. If conspiracy theorists were correct about the Nixon administration's willing to use "any means necessary" to silence their opponents, all bets were off. A lot of people were paranoid, but Lennon had reasons for his fears.

"We had a conversation about musicians who died young," Krassner says, the recent tragedies of Janis Joplin, Jim Morrison, and Jimi Hendrix very much on the minds of the rock community. "I was quoting something that they were all really killed by the CIA or something like that. He said, 'No, no. They were all self-destructive.'"

Lennon's final words to Krassner on the topic left the publisher with chills long after his guests departed: "He said, 'If anything happens to me and Yoko, it wasn't an accident.'"

•   •   •

"YOU'RE A LONG way from New York City," Geraldo Rivera said, and asked a question tailor-made for Lennon. "What brings you here?"

"A car," Lennon deadpanned. He paused, then shared a laugh with Rivera, the old-school punch line echoing Lennon's answer to how he found America eight years earlier: "Turn left at Greenland."

John and Yoko spent most of August 5, 1972, playing tourist with Rivera—by then a New York friend.[3] They had first met in the Village and had seen each other often as the WABC-TV *Eyewitness News* reporter covered both the INS story and Yoko's search for Kyoko. Getting together on the West Coast invited a chance to see some of the city in friendly company and catch up, on the record, about any new developments.

There was a lot to talk about. Lennon's status with immigration remained uncertain, as were the whereabouts of Yoko's daughter. Equally uncertain were Lennon's professional options: freshly stung by the backlash to *Some Time in New York City*, any plans for a concert tour—musical rather than political—awaited visa allowances.

Lennon knew what he didn't plan for during his stay in California: "We don't want to do any politics," he said. "We came down here to get away from that."

Yet the issues were never far from Lennon's mind while John and Yoko wandered with Rivera and a cameraman. They rode the cable cars and gave dozens of passengers a lifetime memory; they walked along the wharf, drove the roller-coaster streets, and stopped at a hillside lookout point for a view of the Golden Gate Bridge. It seemed a good day: bright skies, the wind from the bay blowing strands of Lennon's hair under a beret-style cap, his denim jacket flapping in the breeze. They'd been on the West Coast for several days, had spent the weekend at Krassner's oceanside cabin, and were settled in the Hotel Miyako where Rivera and a skeleton crew recorded off-the-cuff segments for later broadcast.

Guitar in hand while holding a conversation, Lennon played bits and pieces from a mental jukebox stocked over a lifetime. He sang the first two verses of the truly appropriate "Fools Like Me" by Jerry Lee Lewis, a lament of misunderstood romance: "Everybody tells me love is blind / maybe so but I refuse to see." He switched to a tropical "Down in the Caribbean" groove, riffed a few bars of Buddy Holly's "Peggy Sue." Geraldo asked about his influences and personal tastes, which seemed to come from a variety of sources. Many styles, but most from a time when Lennon was discovering his love of music.

"I don't know what the titles are," Lennon said. "I know the song but I don't really know bluegrass from green grass. Everybody remembers their own favorites. I'm just doin' the ones [from] when I first had a rock group."

It always came back to music for Lennon. His forays into political activism were but one aspect of a multifaceted artist,

one who had conquered his chosen field. Rivera wondered where
Lennon's muses would take him next.

"What do you want to do, really want to do, man?" Rivera
asked. "You've done virtually everything, the Beatles. What's
left?"

"We want to pool our heads and do a new form," Lennon said.
"It could be movies, it could be anything. We're always instinc-
tive, we just follow the wind. Like sails on a yacht, when the wind
gets in us we just go with it, you know."

That ship, however, was stuck in a harbor, anchored by court
appearances and legal challenges. Lennon was half-resigned to
being deported, and mostly concerned with the limited options
for Yoko: the courts had awarded her paper custody of Kyoko,
but ex-husband Tony Cox could afford to be patient during the
deportation proceedings. The ordeal left him and Yoko in a state
of tired disbelief.

"You can't believe it's happening to you," Lennon said. "You
never know what the state's doing. The judge said you must
bring the child up in the continent of America, and we're quite
happy with that. We'd love to be here."

If allowed to stay, Rivera asked, would Lennon continue his
active participation in the antiwar movement?

"I don't know what active is," Lennon said. "I'd always look at
every offer to help very thoroughly and decide the pros and cons
of any move or cause. We consider everything. It depends on
what the gigs are, right?"

Rivera had just the gig in mind, a project they'd talked about
for several months. Rivera was equal parts investigative reporter,

fiery activist, and gonzo crusader—and a journalist of unlikely beginnings. After he had graduated from Brooklyn Law School in 1969, Rivera served as an investigator with the New York Police Department, then as counsel for a Puerto Rican activist group, the Young Lords. Television called and Rivera became an on-air reporter with New York's ABC affiliate. In late 1971 he began investigating disturbing allegations about a New York hospital, and did so in decidedly street fashion. As recalled by the *Atlantic* magazine, Rivera "used a stolen key to investigate the Willowbrook State School for the Mentally Retarded. His televised report on the rampant abuse and neglect of the residents led to changes in state law and new standards for the treatment of the mentally disabled across the country."[4]

The Willowbrook story aired in January 1972 and resulted in near-immediate change for patients and long-term improvements for an incalculable number of suffering souls. The Peabody Award–winning exposé put Rivera on the national broadcast map.

There was more to be done, and the Willowbrook reports spawned thoughts of a benefit concert. Rivera's idea, to make a "one-to-one" connection between the people of New York and victims of Willowbrook, was perfectly consistent with what Lennon had been trying to say. The chance to bring both funds and awareness to the cause was exactly what he'd been looking for—to help a local charity, one not likely to spark controversy, and do what he most wanted and missed: get onstage and play some rock and roll for a reason.

As recalled in *Lennon Revealed*, Rivera said that Lennon had been eager to help from the minute he saw the televised reports, and to do more than just make a token appearance onstage.[5] Lennon "was not a celebrity who just loaned his name to a cause," Rivera said. "Both John and Yoko felt like adopted citizens of New York. They wanted to give something back. John was extra sensitive to the needs of others."

•   •   •

LENNON WAS ABSENT in body but present in spirit when the Republican National Convention got underway in Miami on August 21.

A last-minute change found both the Democrats and Republicans convening in Miami: some claimed that hippie pressure forced the GOP move from San Diego; others said a donation by ITT in Florida paved the way. First up in July was the Democratic nomination of George McGovern, whose perhaps too-progressive platform that included abortion rights and gay liberation added a sacrificial lamb–quality to his candidacy. A fair number of activists showed up and hung around Flamingo Park for a few days, but the big show was the following month when the Republicans convened.

The August convention attracted the expected celebrities to either protest or support the Nixon administration, generational lines as clear as ideology: antiwar stars included Shirley MacLaine, Warren Beatty, and fresh-from-North-Vietnam Jane Fonda; support for the president was shown by Jimmy Stewart, Frank Sinatra, and Sammy Davis Jr.

If massive, violent problems had been expected, the convention failed to meet doomsday prophecies, although the week was not without incident: one widely reported clash featured those in support of the president spitting in the faces of disabled Vietnam Veterans Against the War, including one of the group's leading voices, wheelchair-bound Ron Kovic (whose 1976 autobiography *Born on the Fourth of July* would be dramatized in a 1989 film by fellow veteran Oliver Stone). More than two hundred demonstrators were arrested after Miami Police—credited up to that point with emphasizing negotiations over assault tactics—let loose with teargas to end what they considered a small riot. (*Rolling Stone*'s Hunter S. Thompson and reporter Andrea Mitchell were among the gassed when they were assumed to be resisting arrest.)

As expected by the White House and FBI, Jerry Rubin and Abbie Hoffman were present and accounted for, seen on the floor pretending to be reporters on assignment for *Popular Mechanics* magazine, but the words "You're under arrest" were not directed at the Yippies most expected to cause problems. Along with presumably keeping an eye on "Hanoi Jane" Fonda, the FBI made sure that Miami agents and cops knew which of the high-profile radical leaders would most likely cause a problem.

This included John Lennon, who remained an expected visitor to Miami by investigators still determined to find reasons to deport. Attempts to have him arrested for narcotics had failed; either Lennon lived a clean, drug-free life or New York cops made little effort to help the feds.

A memo had been prepared for convention distribution that included a physical description of Lennon—to educate Southern officers as to his identity—with a note that a drug bust might help a fading federal argument: "Local INS has very loose case in NY for deporting subject on narcotics charge in England. INS has stressed to Bureau that if Lennon were to be arrested in US for possession of narcotics he would become more likely to be immediately deportable."[6]

The name John Winston Lennon headlined a be-on-the-lookout poster that was distributed to local law enforcement agencies, and included a by-the-numbers profile of a white Englishman, approximately six feet tall, weighing 160 pounds, brown to blond hair, and the fact that he'd been arrested in his native land for narcotics.

This time a picture was included—unlike previous bureau memos that mentioned the need to have a photo "for identification purposes"—an image of a longhaired man with circular-frame glasses. The photo included a cartoon balloon emerging that had him declaring, "The pope smokes dope."

But the FBI circulated a picture of the wrong man; it was David Peel. The photo was from a publicity release for Peel's comically named album. Some confusion may be allowed—sort of—as the flyer included the names John Lennon and Yoko Ono as producers. But there was very little resemblance between Peel and any former Beatle.

The absence of John Lennon in Florida all but closed the FBI's investigation. His nonappearance was confirmed in an August 30 memo filed by an agent—who went to Miami in undercover capacity as a member of the Weathermen Task Force: Lennon "was not observed by the case agent . . . it is believed the subject did not travel to Miami as he had previously planned." INS attorney Vincent Schiano likewise reported the no-show, and said there was no additional evidence that Lennon was "active in the New Left," a movement that suffered from internal disputes: "The subject has fallen out of the favor of activists Jerry Rubin, Stewart Albert and Rennie Davis, due to the subject's lack of interest in committing himself to involvement in anti-war and New Left activities."

The John Lennon case was placed on "pending inactive status." The New York office sent headquarters a "don't call us, we'll call you" message; they would advise and inform if any changes took place in Lennon's deportation case.

For some Movement leaders there was an empty-tank quality after the convention. Life under the federal microscope took its toll, and Jay Craven returned to DC and the re-relocated offices of a dwindling Coalition for Peace and Justice. Intimidation tactics kept the radicals in check whether in Miami or Washington, and any threat they might have once posed seemed to have dissolved. Craven recalls being tailed and shadowed throughout the convention, and realizing that the Nixon agenda would continue no matter their opposition.

"We were under a lot of surveillance. They had agents in the next office who wanted us to know they were there," Craven says. "The Nixon administration's effort to intimidate and strategically block the Movement won."

Whatever the future held for the coalition and the nearly defunct Yippies, Rennie Davis knew it no longer included John Lennon. In their minds Lennon backed away from the Movement as a whole due to green card concerns; in reality he'd simply distanced himself from Rubin, but kept on fighting. The politically driven concert tour had been a great idea once, the peak of a burgeoning movement. But instead of a victory cheer the Movement seemed ready for a funeral march.

"My initial reaction to John coming out to join us was really colored by the larger context of the enormous role he played," Davis says. "He breathed life into something that had lost its way and was unwinding."

Even without Lennon in their future, Davis wondered if there was any Left remaining to rally at this uncertain threshold.

"Coming off this phenomenon of young people who stepped up to change the world, by Miami it was over," Davis says. "There was one more demonstration outside the White House, but for all practical purposes it was at an end."

• • •

LENNON APPROACHED THE One-to-One benefit concert as more than just a unique performance; the August 30 show was intended to be the first of many.

"I was ready to go on the road for pure fun," Lennon told *Rolling Stone* of his expectations. "I didn't want to go on the road for money. I felt like going on the road and playing music. And whatever excuse—charity or whatever—would have done me."

John and Yoko returned to New York and spent the latter half of August rehearsing with Elephant's Memory—long, hard, and loud; stories are told that initial sessions in a rented space on West Tenth Street they'd christened Butterfly Studios sparked neighbor complaints, so rehearsals continued at the Fillmore East.

Photographer Bob Gruen recalled Lennon embracing the increased rehearsal schedule, and his love for music overcame his performance anxieties. "A spirit of rock 'n' roll really permeated the space," Gruen said.[7] The common denominator of music served as a way to loosen up while getting the show together. Bonding continued during postrehearsal dinners, often at the uptown Home restaurant Lennon had come to enjoy, and on one notable occasion to a Chinatown establishment known to stock a full bar. Gruen said the long night grew longer when Lennon—who had always picked up the group dinner tabs—realized he had no cash on him. Neither did anyone else, and additional rounds of drinks were ordered while they waited for one of John and Yoko's assistants to wake up and bring money.

The final selections would be determined from among dozens of songs the group prepared, running through arrangements over and over. Lennon spoke or whispered as often as he sang to avoid shredding his voice prior to showtime.

Lennon was confident in the music, Adam Ippolito says, at least as far as the band was concerned. The overall sound was enhanced with added thump to the rhythm section: session drummer Jim Keltner served as a second percussionist—a frequent collaborator heard on Lennon's first two post-Beatles albums—along with former Elephant's bassist John Ward.

"By that point he was feeling pretty good," Ippolito says. "We were in a groove playing together. He was ready."

The Elephants needed to be equally prepared. The show represented a marked graduation from what the band had experienced by that point in their career: no matter how enthusiastic the crowds at Max's Kansas City, club dates were a world away from a packed arena audience eager to cheer for a music legend. The band recalls that Lennon and Apple made sure the group's equipment was suitable to the venue—Madison Square and beyond. Lennon, Tex Gabriel recalls, was as quick to spread money on the music as he was contributing to underground newspapers or Leftist ideals.

"There was this guy the Lennons had who carried around this black bag," Gabriel says. "Inside was thousands of dollars in cash; loads of money like from a bank heist or something. John told him to take a certain amount to go get Marshall amps and whatever else we needed. Didn't rent them, just bought them." Bandsmen estimated that Lennon gave upward of $100,000 toward equipment purchases.

"It doesn't sound like a lot now," Van Scyoc says, "but $100,000 in gear at that time was a lot of money." He recalls being impressed by the quality of equipment, which clearly indicated plans beyond the benefit show. This is the moment the Elephants had been waiting for, to go on the road for Lennon's debut tour as a solo artist.

"When the thing came up we thought, 'Thank God: a gig!' We jumped all over that," Van Scyoc says. "We definitely hadn't been playing venues like the Garden with the Elephants, that's for sure. We were in front of three thousand seniors once, but this was very high profile, about as high as you can get."

More than a just a show, the "Concert to Free the Children of Willowbrook"—as originally called in *Billboard* magazine—was the climax to "One-to-One Day" in New York City, so declared by

Mayor John Lindsay. Lennon's involvement was not restricted to rehearsal and stage time: he and Yoko joined fifteen thousand Willowbrook volunteers and patients for a preshow picnic in Central Park, where the Sheep Meadow played host to games, music, hot-air balloon rides, and encounters with a wandering Beatle.

Intentionally, there was limited fanfare at the picnic. Lennon found the balance he'd sought of using his celebrity to help a cause yet remaining one of a crowd, not the spotlit leader—a focus that would be unavoidable when they hit the stage.

•   •   •

"WELCOME TO THE rehearsal," Lennon greeted the afternoon crowd, fifteen-thousand strong in Madison Square Garden for the first of two shows.[8]

On a no-frills stage that barely made room for musicians and amplifiers, harsh spotlights brightened Lennon's round blue eyeglasses; he'd dressed Village casual in an olive-green US Army shirt that bore sergeant's stripes, a Second Infantry Division patch, and the name *Reinhardt*. But despite his outward displays of confidence, the Elephants knew that Lennon was more than a little nervous. There was a lot at stake for him, to prove his worth with new material that had met mixed reactions, and—as all four former Beatles had to come to terms with—expectations as to what he'd play. Everyone had certain hopes, including the Elephants. Gary Van Scyoc recalls preshow discussions regarding the set list.

"We wanted to do a ton of Beatles songs," Van Scyoc says. "But he only allowed us to do 'Come Together.' We rehearsed about ten, but that was a cool one, we got off on that."

The band enjoyed the chance to play a brief set as one of the concert's opening acts—along with Sha Na Na, Roberta Flack, Melanie, and Stevie Wonder, all of whom performed gratis for the cause. The spotlight, however, was clear, as were hopes for a little musical nostalgia.

"We're going back to the past *just* once," Lennon emphasized before launching into "Come Together."

Lennon may have jinxed himself when he told the crowd, "You probably remember this better than I do . . . something about a flattop." Sure enough, the lyrical wordplay he sang that began with "Here come old flattop"—a song composed of fragmented imagery—didn't quite match the *Abbey Road* recording known so well by the fans. A few stumbles here and there: "over you" rather than "over me"; he didn't seem sure if he had hair "under," "beneath," or "below" his knees. Each misstep produced a visible grimace.

"I nearly got all the words right," Lennon said at song's end. He shook his head as he sat at a piano. "I'll have to stop writing those daft words, man; I don't know what I'm saying. I'm getting old."

The bandsmen held up their end of the musical ship, doing their damnedest not to disappoint Lennon. Adam Ippolito says that the hour-plus performance was clearly a different and greater pressure than doing one or two quick songs on TV.

"He was self-conscious and didn't like the fact that there was a mistake or two," Ippolito says. "Most people didn't notice."

The set list allowed the band to demonstrate its own place in Lennon's musical life with selections from *Some Time in New*

York City, and not just serve as stand-ins for Paul, George, and Ringo. "New York City" was a surefire crowd-pleaser at the Garden, and one of five *Some Time* songs along with "Woman Is the Nigger of the World," "Sisters O Sisters," "Born in a Prison," and "We're All Water."

Lennon's first two post-Beatles albums were well represented: "Imagine" was "one of the supreme songs of the set," Van Scyoc recalls. Lennon had familiar songs to offer from his solo repertoire: "Instant Karma," a blistering "Cold Turkey," and a singalong "Give Peace a Chance," which featured the audience banging tambourines they'd been given at the door. For a lesser-known number, "Well, Well, Well," Lennon playfully told the crowd it was "a song from one of the albums I made since leaving the Rolling Stones."

Nerves aside, Lennon had fun. The biggest grin he wore that night was during a rowdy rip-up of Elvis Presley's "Hound Dog." Lennon and Gabriel danced with their guitars; Stan Bronstein grabbed a girl and twisted his beefy way through the song, old-time rock and roll at its finest. The Beatles were known to kick-start recording sessions with a romp through tunes they played in the Cavern days, a habit Lennon continued with the Elephants.

"When rehearsing we used to do those songs just to warm up," Van Scyoc says. "It wasn't like a conscious thing, but we got him in a groove doing that stuff. We pulled out old Chuck Berry songs, always reverting back to that old '50s stuff. Whenever John really wanted to relax, that's where he'd go."

The One-to-One show captured moments of pure Lennon, the essence of his life as an artist. While the show was named for its humanitarian cause, Lennon made that personal connection in ways few musicians could. He remained one of the most soul-baring singer-songwriters to ever form an intimate relationship with an audience. Not many would write a song like "Mother"; fewer still would perform it in such stark capacity. A lonely spotlight, spare piano chords, a singular wounded voice revealed Lennon's deepest pain to thousands of friends:

> *Mother . . . you had me, but I never had you;*
> *Father, you left me, but I never left you.*
> *So . . . I . . . I just want to tell you . . . Good-bye.*

"He absolutely put it all out there," Gabriel says. What the audience saw gave similar chills to the guitarist standing ten feet away from Lennon. "It was raw, and it was real. Very real. There was no pretense with him."

Any fault, Lennon freely said, lay with his own performance, the rough edges heard at times that afternoon and evening. Separate from a critical analysis of the music, Lennon gave every impression of wanting to get back out there and do it better.

"We'll get it right next time," Lennon said near the end of the show, a brief nod to the random flaws likely unheard by the audience.

Next time never happened. John Lennon never again played a full concert, never again headlined marquees around the country or world. Other than a few brief, one- or two-song performances scattered over the next two years, Lennon's 1972 Madison Square Garden shows were the warm-ups for a tour unfinished, a legacy of songs unheard.

•   •   •

IN A CERTAIN regard the One-to-One concerts were an unqualified success. A tremendous amount of good resulted from the
overall attention and awareness generated by Rivera, an incalculable amount of assistance to patients and families over the
years. Lennon was aware of the recent history of rock charities
being taken to the cleaners, as was alleged with Allen Klein
and George Harrison's Bangladesh benefit; he said during the
show that he hoped the donated money reached its intended
beneficiary.

It did. Funds from the concert went to three New York charities that built residences for Willowbrook patients and others
with similar needs. ABC paid a reported $300,000 for the rights
to film and broadcast the event, and negotiations began for an
album. More than $1.5 million would be generated over time
from broadcast revenue and record sales. The $60,000 contribu-
tion to the cause that Lennon made when he purchased tickets
for patients and caregivers was left out of FBI reports that speculated on Lennon's contributions to questionable beneficiaries.

At the time, the critical reception from music fans and reviewers was mixed. The star attraction was duly praised, but Lennon
was again angered at the eagerness by some to publicly deride
Yoko, who had a few too many vocal spots in the eyes of her
detractors.

"Everyone loved the band," Gary Van Scyoc recalls. "But it was
a little too much of her and it just rubbed people the wrong way."

Not every critic jumped on the anti-Yoko bandwagon.

Writing for *Soul Sounds* magazine, Toby Mamis was among her supporters.[9]

"A lot of people don't get off on Yoko Ono's music," Mamis said. "I think she's taking rock in new directions and we should go with her and see what she discovers. A lot of ostriches like to keep their heads in the sand and pretend things will always be this way and that ain't true. Someone's got to find out where we turn next and Yoko, among others, is looking."

Mamis reminded skeptics that this was Lennon's first major production on his own, and that Elephant's Memory—"one hell of a good hard rock group"—was the first stable team of players Lennon worked with since the Beatles, a band that Lennon recorded with, rehearsed, "planned and sweated with the anticipation of a live concert."

Rolling Stone's conclusion was mixed: "His performance was a fresh reminder of what everybody had known all along, that he is a startlingly good songwriter and a strong, intelligent, expressive singer." Lennon "appeared to be having a great time," and even "managed to get some life into 'Woman Is the Nigger of the World,' an awful, lapel-grabbing song, the political rectitude of which never compensates for [bad lyrics]."

Years later, in 1986, *Rolling Stone*'s David Fricke looked back on the show when a videotape of the concert was released.[10] Fricke appreciated the gems in the rough, and applauded the "soulful gusto of Lennon's singing" and "the surprising breadth of his set list." He praised Elephant's Memory—"the left-wing New York club band"—for solid work. The Madison Square Garden concert would be remembered as much for its rarity as its intent. "Classic

Lennon," Fricke called it. "Because it's all here—his humor, pain, anger and unshakable faith in the power of rock & roll to change the world."

•   •   •

THE ELEPHANTS PLAYED one final performance with Lennon on September 6 for the Labor Day Jerry Lewis telethon. The annual benefit for muscular dystrophy seemed an odd platform for Lennon—arguably more so than Mike Douglas—given Lewis's usual guest list of old-guard entertainment in the style of former partner Dean Martin, Frank Sinatra, and other Las Vegas luminaries.

Not that Lennon adapted his style: sunglasses in place, hair flowing in a variety of directions, Lennon first sang "Imagine" before the band rallied the studio audience into joining a reggae-tinted version of "Give Peace a Chance."

"Send money now . . ." Lennon sang in between title chants to get the phones ringing.

Many speculated that Lennon's brief appearance—coming so soon on the heels of the benefit concert—was designed to curry favor with the government. Doubtful, says Gary Van Scyoc. Lennon was consistent with his views and plans. Critical barbs didn't dampen Lennon's eagerness to get back on tour; Lennon believed the deportation effort was based on his peace promotion, which he also continued.

Van Scyoc recalls the band and Lennon growing equally impatient about touring. They'd started their relationship less than a year earlier from *Mike Douglas* to the recording studio and Madison Square Garden, getting everyone ready for something that just wasn't happening.

"It was just boom-boom-boom at a thousand miles an hour," Van Scyoc says. "You think it's going to go on forever and, okay, we'll be patient. Nobody knew the green card issue was going to take years."

Securing his residency would prove a long, frustrating ordeal. The deportation case stalled in court, and motions from attorney Leon Wildes worked their way into a system of extended deadlines, adjournments, and delays. There seemed little threat that he'd be kicked out, but Lennon was unable to leave the country for fear of being blocked Charlie Chaplin–style from reentry. His now-extended visitor's visa allowed only limited options for what he could do professionally; he could record and perform, but not for a fee.

Although his case was now considered a low priority, there seemed little interest in pushing the matter to a conclusion and Lennon was left in legal limbo. Media attention faded due to the non-newsworthiness of adjournments and extensions, and Wildes realized they were in for a long wait: "They were afraid if they dismissed it they would be accused from the other side of being too lenient," Wildes says. "So it just hung out there, they didn't know what to do with him. They had wanted him out at one time and now they couldn't care less."

CHAPTER 7

"YOU CAN'T KEEP A GOOD BAND DOWN"

"People have got to know whether or not their president is a crook. Well, I am not a crook."

—RICHARD M. NIXON,
    November 1973

LENNON CONTINUED TO feel the relentless pressure of fighting the immigration department, of being under watch, but there was more to it. He would tell *Rolling Stone* two years later that the myriad legal issues, professional uncertainty, and the ongoing search for Yoko's daughter took a toll.[1]

"It was really getting to me," Lennon said. "Not only was I physically having to appear in court cases, it just seemed like a toothache . . . a permanent toothache. There was a period where I just couldn't function, you know? I was so paranoid from them tappin' the phone and followin' me. How could I prove that they were tappin' me phone?"

Life under surveillance was one more restriction, coupled with and causing Lennon's inability to schedule tour dates. Reviews of the Madison Square Garden show heightened Lennon's desire to "get it right next time," and the perpetual "toothache" left him uncomfortable and irritable that fall. In early October he told the *New Musical Express* that criticism of his musical direction being "self-indulgent" was getting old: "It's only because I'm not doing what they want me to do," Lennon said. "They're still hung up on my past. People talk about not what you do, but how you do it, which is like discussing how you dress or if your hair is long or short."[2]

Some appointments had to be kept, like obligations as producer of the Apple-issued *Elephant's Memory* album. Lennon tried to sidestep the spotlight when Apple introduced the band and album at an early October press party. Special guests included Mignon, a six-month-old baby elephant that roamed the room, "painted up like a Lower East Side groupie for the occasion," *Rolling Stone* reported.[3] The Lennon connection, however, remained prominent; the band was introduced as "the working-class heroes we've all been waiting for." Lennon's actual presence on the record was limited to some backing vocals and rhythm guitar work, but his shadow remained too large to ignore, and not necessarily to the band's benefit. Apple hosted the one event and scheduled brief tours of the Midwest and in California, but with Lennon unable to headline a series of concerts, bassist Gary Van Scyoc says that neither the producer nor label seemed able to give the time and attention needed by a relatively unknown band. It wasn't a problem Lennon had experienced in recent memory.

"Being on Apple was a big thrill for the first month," Van Scyoc says. "Until we went up there and started looking for the promotion department. There was no promotions department. The Beatles put out an album and it just sold and sold. But the Elephants needed help. Basically we signed with a label that had no facilities to promote us. It was a good thing, but it wasn't going out."

Elephant's Memory was very much the band's creation—but Lennon had enthusiastically put backing vocals and rhythm guitar on some selections; he added a piano piece to Van Scyoc's "Wind Ridge," a collaboration the bassist fondly recalls.

"John loved my tune, 'Wind Ridge,' and wrote piano lines," Van Scyoc says. "On the record it's just John, myself, and Jim Keltner on the track. He sent the rest of the Elephants home that night."

The album cover itself painted a grim picture, with a moody black-and-white landscape that contrasted with earlier hippie-era imagery. Founders Stan Bronstein and Rick Frank wrote the bulk of its songs—other than "Wind Ridge" and "Life" by Tex Gabriel—which mixed autobiography with the band's signature politics. The group's identity was addressed in a semidefiant song by Frank, "Local Plastic Ono Band," and the guitar-driven "Chuck 'n' Bo," a salute to Berry and Diddley after the two legends had shared stage time with the band.

The band's reputation may have preceded the album,

regardless of the quality of the music. By late 1972, political rock had lost much of its edge, and Apple's promotion of "working-class hero" musicians—well represented in "Liberation Special" and "Power Boogie"—made them difficult to market. Some tried to champion the Elephant's talent.

"Forget the bullshit and listen to the music," advised *Melody Maker*: "They pour beautiful guitar from Wayne Gabriel and wild sax from Stan Bronstein. Listen to Gabriel take off like a sky rocket on 'Chuck 'n' Bo.'"[4]

The consensus was that Lennon's faith in the band had been justified: New York writers familiar with the group wanted to like the album, although they too wondered if revolution rock was still relevant, or would be again. *Village Voice* writer Richard Nusser said the sound may not have hit the right notes for the times: "A thundering expression of rage that's either four years too late, or four years too early."[5]

The critics favored Lennon's "discovery," but magazine writers don't buy all the records. *Cash Box* speculated on the album's sales potential: "This album will be testing grounds for their live excitement translating itself to record sales."[6]

The translation fell short. The LP briefly approached but couldn't crack the *Billboard* Top 200, and no single caught the fancy of the record-buying public. Was Lennon's endorsement of the band as rockers for the revolution a mixed blessing? Gabriel says the sudden national exposure was built on two associations—the Yippies and Lennon—that came wrapped in the same package.

"Sometimes I wondered about that, but if we hadn't been

such a political band would Jerry Rubin have been involved?"
Gabriel asks. "Would Lennon have been interested if we were just
another rock and roll band? Our political outlook had a lot to do
with all of it happening."

Maybe music for the masses had already had its share of hippie history. Cynical minds said that music just didn't matter anymore. Rock and roll had sold out, *Rolling Stone*'s Nick Tosches
said, and everyone might be better off remembering that when
listening to the album.[7] It was "completely ludicrous" to think
that the music mattered as a sociopolitical force.

"Elephant's Memory is just a fuckin' band and the album is
just plain old fuckin' music," Tosches concluded. "The artists
and media of rock's aging counterculture have been so com-
fortably incorporated into the bloodstream of traditional big
business economics as to render the mere concept of any viably
revolutionary nature absurd."

If "Movement music" was passé, Lennon's blessing of the
band may have been trumped, Tosches said, by their alliances with "such color sergeants of the revolution as Jerry
Rubin . . . and renowned stupid person David Peel. Elephant's
Memory are commonly thought of as being part of the great revolutionary consortium's going-out-of-business-sale."

Whatever the band was, in the eyes of many fans the stage
area near Lennon was forever reserved for other musicians. In
the wake of the critical response to the Madison Square Garden
shows, Lennon realized that his onstage collaborations—with
Yoko or the Elephants—were destined to be measured against a
particular standard.

"I've got used to the fact—just about—that whatever I do is going to be compared to the other Beatles," Lennon said. "If I took up ballet dancing, my ballet dancing would be compared with Paul's bowling. But I've come to learn something big . . . I cannot let the Top Ten dominate my art. If my worth is only to be judged by whether I'm in the Top Ten or not, then I'd better give up."

By November 1972 Lennon's immersion in radical politics wasn't the same as it had been a year earlier. He didn't change his pro-peace views—and didn't back down from fighting for the chance to perform political songs. Another time, another year, and the partnership with Elephant's Memory might well have continued to evolve along with current events, the musicians exploring a sound as well as a message, but too many extenuating factors stood in the way. Reflecting on it years later Lennon said the two motivating factors went hand in hand.[8]

"The last thing on earth I want to do is perform," Lennon said. "That's a direct result of the immigration thing. In '71, '72, I wanted to go out and rock me balls off onstage and I just stopped."

And his role in the Movement? His revolution-inspired forays into writing as if on assignment as self-proclaimed musical journalist ran contrary to his artistic vision. "The art is more important than the thing and sometimes I have to remind meself of it." The year he'd spent with the Yippies and the Elephants had been productive by output standards, but lacking in Lennon's own self-assessment.

"I was still putting out the work," Lennon said. "But in the back of me head it was: What do you want to be? What are you looking for? I'm a freakin' artist, man, not a fuckin' race horse."

•　　•　　•

ELECTION NIGHT, OF November 7, 1972, was not—by all accounts—one of John Lennon's finest. So many things came to a crashing halt with the president's overwhelming reelection win with the thought of four more years under Nixonian rule, there was no reason to think Lennon's life and career shouldn't follow suit.

John, Yoko, and the Elephants were in the studio that fall to record Yoko's ambitious two-disc LP, *Approximately Infinite Universe*, the final piece of their three-part contract with Apple. Since it was election night, sessions had begun early, half-hearted renditions at best, and came to an early end. Nobody felt like playing music: a recording session suddenly seemed pointless, as did a lot of things.

There had been little suspense that Nixon would win as he claimed more than 60 percent of the popular vote, one of the largest victory margins in presidential history. In the electoral contest Nixon all but swept the national board by winning every state except Massachusetts, and the District of Columbia. A generation felt defeated, and Lennon had some renewed personal concerns: given what seemed a mandate of the people, would the president's men decide now to finish the deportation process?

Gary Van Scyoc recalls a disgusted Lennon calling a halt to playing. An election-night blowout at Jerry Rubin's Village apartment seemed an appropriate place to drink away the evening's sorrows.

"It was really deflating," Van Scyoc says. "A whole lot of drinking going on, even before we left the studio. John's not a great drinker, as everybody knows. The party was already a disaster waiting to happen."

As recounted in Jon Wiener's *Come Together* and recalled by the Elephants, Rubin answered the door to a John Lennon "crazy with rage," cursing and screaming.[9] Lennon took in the apartment filled with would-be revolutionaries; he considered his host, whose leadership of a movement was now a memory.

Lennon ranted, a drunken tirade of class warfare and lost causes. He had grown tired of the politics as preached by Rubin—by a lot of people—and frustrated by that old familiar feeling that he was being used. And for what? There was no hope, Lennon said; these people couldn't do anything, couldn't protect themselves against the forces of Nixon and the man.

Who was gonna do it? Lennon asked. Was anyone in that room ready to take responsibility for their lives, or were they waiting for some savior to show them the way?

Their answer was: Lennon. In spite of Nixon's victory, Stan Bronstein said it was up to Lennon to revive the Movement.

"You, John," Bronstein said. "They'll listen to you."

That may have been the final straw, an echo of demands that began early in Beatlemania, of fans wanting more than just music. There had been times when parents brought ill or disabled children to concerts and begged for backstage access in hopes that a touch from a Beatle might—somehow, in some way—provide more than just hope. Lennon—the leader of the Beatles—was expected to have all the answers for a generation: What clothes should we wear? they asked. How long should our hair be? What drugs were okay? What religions were okay?

In New York he wanted to be just one of the crowd, but he was never just one of the crowd. He was John Lennon, head of the most influential entertainment force in history. Revolutionaries from every movement and cause wanted more than a casual endorsement: they wanted Lennon to lead them in the march to a better future. He'd given his time, money, and fame to Rubin, the Yippies, John Sinclair, and in return had telephones tapped, threats of deportation, and life spent under federal watch. The Movement, Lennon said, needed another solution.

"They haven't been listening to me," Lennon scowled.

Lennon was not a happy drunk, and Van Scyoc recalls a bad scene in the making. "John was making a lot of noise and being generally unruly," Van Scyoc says. "I was glad to get out of there, to be honest."

The party crowd thinned past midnight. Lennon drunkenly flirted with a woman he soon took into a bedroom, his actions no secret to anyone in the room, including Yoko. The closed door did not block what obviously took place.

Bronstein discreetly turned up the radio's volume to mask the noise; Tex Gabriel sat at Yoko's side, gave her his sunglasses to hide tearful eyes, and made small talk while the party came to an ugly end.

The country seemed destined to four more years of Richard Nixon's presidency. Far less certain was the state of Lennon's residency, John and Yoko's marriage, his partnership with the Elephants, his career, and his mental state.

•　　•　　•

WHILE LENNON SHARED album space with Yoko Ono on *Some Time in New York City*—a near fifty-fifty songwriting partnership—*Approximately Infinite Universe* was very much Yoko's solo album; Lennon's involvement was limited to a few backing vocals, some guitar work, and a producer credit. The early recording sessions that were interrupted on election night stayed in limbo for several days as Lennon scrambled to apologize and repair a seemingly broken marriage. The bulk of the album would be recorded at New York's Record Plant studios, but by Thanksgiving Elephant's Memory had flown to California for several performances and John and Yoko split time between Texas—and the ongoing search for Kyoko—and the West Coast, where some sessions for the album were held.

Musically, the Elephants enjoyed the creativity of putting blues-based backup to Yoko's feminist poetry. Gary Van Scyoc calls Yoko "one of the most interesting artists I ever worked with," and that it was her guidance—not Lennon's—that aimed for a more pop-rock approach than her previous experimental tracks.

"We revamped the chord structures to be more Elephant's Memory compatible," Van Scyoc says. "It was actually a fun project, and the bottom line was that Yoko really did have a vision of what she wanted."

Lennon believed the Elephant's capable of the project, one
that could have tested the talents or patience of other musicians.
Tex Gabriel told Calliope Kurtz, sometime music critic and feminist who wrote "The Feminist Songs of Yoko Ono," that the band
was able to meet both producers' expectations.[10]

"John had faith in us to do it," Gabriel says. "We were pretty
experienced by that time, and Yoko had faith in us, too."

In Los Angeles the bandsmen were provided with accom-
modations at the Century Plaza Hotel. Good times in sunny
California for the boys, who compensated for holiday homesick
thoughts by inviting more than fifty people to a Thanksgiving
blowout. Gary Van Scyoc proudly says the Elephants "were the
only band to run up a bigger bill than the Rolling Stones."

Lennon was around for several tracks, Van Scyoc says, but it
was clear that the relationship was fading and that they would
never again share a stage. He was there in spirit as supportive
friend, though. Van Scyoc recalls a memorable show the Elephants played at the Los Angeles Coliseum, a bill that included
the Bee Gees, Cher, and Sly and the Family Stone, which featured
an onstage boost from Lennon.

"John and Yoko called in to introduce us over the PA system,"
Van Scyoc says. "The crowd went crazy. That's a heck of a way to
start a set: had them in our pocket before we even played a note.
It was great."

Lennon wanted to be there, Van Scyoc says, perhaps join the
band onstage, but the timing for Lennon and the Elephants was
not in the cards. During the five weeks the Elephants spent in
California, John and Yoko were again tracking down possible

leads as to Kyoko's whereabouts and scrambled between New York, Texas, and Los Angeles.

Lennon's parting with the Elephants was, if not inevitable, perhaps mutual in some regards. The band struggled, in odd ways, under a Lennon-generated spotlight. Critics may have advised that the band's own album was worth a listen, but media attention inevitably circled back to Lennon. The three younger bandsmen fully hoped to capitalize on the professional opportunity, but Bronstein and Frank retained some feelings that being too famous meant being a sellout. Their respect for Lennon stopped short of sucking-up to a star, and the band hadn't tried to abuse Lennon's friendship; the end of the ride had nothing to do with how they related personally.

The band's political identity seemed to be fading as well. Their association with Jerry Rubin seemed too dominant in Frank's assessment of their future, and relations had cooled considerably between Lennon and the Yippies, and within the radical ranks, to include its long-loyal troubadors.[11]

"There is no Movement," Frank snarled. "We were bozoed on that. I'm not into endorsing any political groups at all." Everyone was at odds with each other, Frank said, and when the Elephants played benefits they found support from some—the Black Panthers or Young Lords—yet scorn from others.

"The women's libbers would yell, 'Sexist, macho bastards,' and we'd get pissed off," Frank said. "That's just where the 'Movement' was at."

Frank and Bronstein told *Rolling Stone* they wanted to be "more than a Plastic Ono band," but a possible direction forward remained unclear. The opportunity was exactly what the younger players—Gabriel, Van Scyoc, and Ippolito—had hoped for, but *Cavalier*'s Lenny Kaye wondered why founders Stan Bronstein and Rick Frank seemed reluctant to cash in.[12]

"They're a funny group, the Memory," Kaye observed. "Proud and not a little hard-headed, and where most other bands would be content to bask in the reflected stardom of the Lennons, the Elephants have steadfastly held to the concept that they're nobody's band but their own."

The Elephants ended their recording work on *Approximately Infinite Universe* as 1972 drew to an end. The third and final piece of their Apple contract didn't improve the band's chances to ride the Lennons' waves to success. The album was released in January 1973 to limited sales—sneaking into the Top 200 at 193—and the predictable harsh reviews published in February and March. The band earned kudos, but Yoko's vocals once again proved too challenging for critics, as did lyrics that ranged from feminist issues to attempts at a more commercial sound. Lennon seemed resigned to few critics paying attention to his wife's work, with those that did offering mostly unsympathetic commentary. In another era Yoko's music would be better appreciated—her musical influence was seen a decade later in postpunk bands such as the B-52s, who freely acknowledged that the origins of their unique sound included Yoko's work.

Perhaps more telling in Nick Tosches' *Rolling Stone* review was an increasingly common feeling among cultural observers that it was perhaps time to mothball the spiritual-Aquarian overtones of a now-bygone era.[13]

"What is this search for meaning, anyway?" Tosches wondered. "Didn't that go out in '68?"

The release of *Approximately Infinite Universe* closed the books on the band's association with Lennon, who remained stuck in immigration limbo and unable to schedule dates or tours. Van Scyoc says he understood that ride wasn't going to last forever.

"It came to a standstill," Van Scyoc says. Equipment valued at six figures would be returned, and regular salaries discontinued. "We were on retainer, but there were weeks when I was rehearsing with Neil Sedaka and collecting John's salary. It was kind of silly for Apple to keep spending money on us every week. He had to cut us loose."

Back in New York, a courier showed up at each of the Elephants' doors one early spring morning bearing a letter sealed in wax, an unnecessary yet theatrical gesture separate from official paperwork that followed from Apple. A personal message, five copies of the "parting of the ways" letter that Van Scyoc remembers fondly for its good spirit, grace, and humor. With true regrets Lennon said the gig was over, but he knew they'd soldier on and take the world by storm.

"You can't keep a good band down," Lennon cheered, and explained that "because of the green card and Apple up in the air," he would be in Los Angeles for a while:

> It's costing too much bread to keep you "on retainer" and I/we have no plans to tour or anything . . . I hope you enjoyed yourselves (we did), your names known enough now to keep you going. See you round, love John and Yoko.

•   •   •

IN A MARCH 1973 deportation order, Lennon was once again ordered to depart the country within sixty days.[14] The paper chase continued even after its motivations were moot. The FBI had officially closed its file; the bureau's final report in December indicated that Lennon and the Yippies had parted ways, with Lennon the jilted radical partner: "In view of subject's inactivity in Revolutionary Activities and his seemingly rejection by NY Radicals, captioned case is being closed in the NY division."

The attempt to deport Lennon, however, had worked its way into a system that couldn't be stopped; untangling the red tape was a process that would outlast the presidential administration that started it. As White House staff scrambled to explain who knew what and when they knew it, the Lennon deportation attempt put INS district director Sol Marks in the uncomfortable position of kicking out a beloved cultural figure. It was the government's right to do so, Marks said at a March 24 press conference, even if they didn't really want to. Marks stressed that while the decision was based on the 1968 marijuana conviction, it was one step in a long process, and the order did not necessarily mean that Lennon would leave soon; he "might thus be able to stay in the US for years as he goes through due process."

The order included an offer of sorts: if Lennon voluntarily left the country, "he might be able to return" under a similar visa to the one issued in 1971, provided a waiver could be obtained for the marijuana conviction. Lennon was effectively being asked to go away for a while and trust the INS and the Nixon administration to do the right thing.

"Having just celebrated our fourth wedding anniversary," Lennon said in a responding statement that was quoted widely, "we are not prepared to sleep in separate beds."

Lennon held a press conference of his own at the offices of the New York City Bar Association. Lennon appeared in the Stimson Room before a crowd of New York attorneys, wearing a badge that read: *Not Insane*. America, Lennon reflected, was "a place to be in, rather than just scoot in and out with the loot." His wife, he said, taught him to love the US, New York in particular, and its ideas of freedom.

Seated at a table with Yoko and Leon Wildes, Lennon said the occasion for which they were gathered that day was to announce the birth of a nation: Nutopia, for which John and Yoko were the first ambassadors. Lennon then read the "Declaration of Nutopia," which he said would duly grant him diplomatic immunity from further deportation hearings:

> *We announce the birth of a conceptual country, NUTOPIA.*
>
> *Citizenship of the country can be obtained by declaration of your awareness of NUTOPIA.*
>
> *NUTOPIA has no land, no boundaries, no passports, only people.*
>
> *NUTOPIA has no laws other than cosmic.*

> *All people of NUTOPIA are ambassadors of the country.*
>
> *As two ambassadors of NUTOPIA, we ask for diplomatic immunity and recognition in the United Nations of our country and its people.*

The day of the Nutopia announcement was, of course, April Fool's Day, with the signed declaration containing a return address from the Nutopian Embassy at One White Street. (The address of the Tribeca townhouse built in the 1800s may have been chosen at random, yet forty years later remained a destination for letters of peace and support addressed to Yoko.) Lennon waved a white handkerchief—the Nutopian flag—to conclude the bit of theater, a surrender that was mostly but not entirely a joke.

But Lennon wasn't giving up, or going away quickly. The sixty days came and went and he remained on American soil, although no longer keeping company with the Elephants or downtown radicals. In April 1973, John and Yoko became the newest residents of the storied Dakota apartment building at West Seventy-Second Street and Central Park West. The building itself boasted considerable screen time as a frequent backdrop in movies, most notably *Rosemary's Baby*; the Dakota's long list of celebrity tenants included at the time Roberta Flack, Lauren Bacall, and Leonard Bernstein. A change of scenery was in order, one that hopefully left behind the days of electronic surveillance.

•   •   •

JOHN AND YOKO maintained a relatively low profile as they settled into their new home, dramatically scaled back from the previous year's flurry of activity and appearances. One public outing took place in early May, when they obtained the hottest tickets of the season to watch a day's worth of Watergate testimony courtesy of Democratic Senator Sam Ervin—a key player in the prosecution of Nixon and his administration—and made a quick in-and-out visit to Washington.[15] Lennon extended his appreciation in a follow-up letter in late June: "Thank you very much for your kindness in arranging our visit to the historic Watergate Hearings," Lennon wrote. "We've been following it on TV—but there's nothing like the 'real thing.' We apologize for leaving without saying goodbye—we had to escape rather quickly! We would have loved to have met Senator Ervin, but thought his time was occupied with more serious matters! Perhaps another time . . ."

In July the Lennons attended the one-year anniversary party for Gloria Steinem's *Ms.* magazine. Guests at the party—a boat ride up and down the Hudson and East rivers for an elongated circle around Manhattan—barely noticed the two. But aside from these brief appearances, a more isolated Lennon spent the summer working on his next album, *Mind Games*, which was recorded in July and August at the Record Plant. He gave only a few scattered interviews after the Nutopia press conference until that fall when it was time to start promoting the album.

Lennon returned to effectively "solo" status with the record.

He took the producer's chair himself rather than offer a return engagement to Phil Spector, and brought in guitarist David Spinozza and old friend Jim Keltner on drums. No Plastic Ono incarnation or Elephants, no shared credits with his wife—marital tensions born the previous November were nearing critical mass. As recalled in *Lennon in America*, the album was "an interim record between being a manic political lunatic and back to being a musician again."[16]

The album mostly steered clear of politics, at least in terms of protest anthems or topical bits of musical journalism, but "Bring on the Lucie (Freeda Peeple)" has been called Lennon's last great protest song, its lyrics clearly bringing an end to Lennon's active involvement:

> *Well we were caught with our hands in the air*
> *Don't despair paranoia is everywhere*
> *We can shake it with love when we're scared*
> *So let's shout it aloud like a prayer*

Lennon often dismissed claims that his songs held greater depth and meaning—even after years of having reviewers and fans scrutinize his thoughts. In the song "Intuition" Lennon offered one explanation for his role as both artist and activist: "My intentions are good, I use my intuition, it takes me for a ride."

Yet *Mind Games* may have included Lennon's final thoughts on the Movement, the revolution, the lessons learned. Lennon restated and affirmed his philosophies in the title song, originally called "Make Love, Not War"—the phrase echoing the song's ending—which Lennon knew was by then an overused cliché. "Mind Games" featured one of Lennon's finest post-Beatles vocal performances and a positive message free of any bitterness that may have built up by then.

"Some call it magic," Lennon said, "to search for the Grail." Positive energies over angry rebellion: "Yes . . . is the answer." A string of phrases formed a consistent picture: "Chanting the mantra of peace on earth; faith in the future out of the now; raising the spirit of peace and love."

The song was well received when released in November. But overall the album met reviews similar to those for *Some Time in New York City*; *Rolling Stone* said the LP included "his worst writing yet."[17] Commercially, however, the record returned Lennon to respectable sales: the album cracked the Top 10, and the title single the Top 20.

Critical backlash couldn't target Yoko, who did not perform on the album but was present as a topic: the musical chronicle of John and Yoko continued with "Aisumasen (I'm Sorry)"; Lennon borrowed a Japanese phrase of apology to beg Yoko's forgiveness for the sad ending to election night at Jerry Rubin's apartment.

The apology wasn't enough to heal a wounded marriage. By the time *Mind Games* was in stores Lennon was back on the West Coast, unable to tour, too tired to fight. Lennon had gone to Los Angeles in October after he and Yoko agreed to separate for an indefinite period. He wouldn't see Yoko again for more than a year.

•   •   •

THE START OF what John Lennon later called his "lost weekend" of California partying weren't his prettiest days, but there was a lot of that going around. The climate in Lennon's adopted home country wasn't promising.

In November 1973, President Richard Nixon felt compelled to address the growing number of questions and suspicions about his administration; during a rare Nixon press conference with the managing editors of the Associated Press, the president answered Watergate questions. That brief speech included one of the most repeated sentences in political history.

Nixon had never once profited from his life in public service, he said. He "earned every cent," and had never mislead the public or obstructed justice: "I welcome this kind of examination, because people have got to know whether or not their president is a crook. Well, I am not a crook."

The humorists had a field day: "Not a crook" became the national punch line in a comedy that would take months to unfold.

Despite Lennon's unequivocal feelings about Nixon, he had lost interest in composing political songs, writing words for the Movement. Lennon knew there was no Movement to speak of anymore, but where exactly he would go was one of many unresolved questions. At the top of that list was a matter of far more importance to Lennon than any music, politics, or business: his separation from Yoko, his wife and constant, day-in, day-out companion of several years.

"As a friend says, I went out for coffee and some papers and I didn't come back," Lennon later said of the separation and fleeing New York.[18] "It's not a matter of who broke it up. It broke up."

Lennon was accompanied by May Pang, who had been a personal assistant of the Lennons. Pang was sent by Yoko to keep an eye on Lennon and, as has been often chronicled, to serve as sexual surrogate while John ran wild on the West Coast—to keep him honest in his cheating during a nearly yearlong party.

It was, as Lennon often described, the extended bachelor party that only a top-level rock-and-roll star could have. A Los Angeles duplex hosted a barroom roundtable of some of the hardest-drinking musicians in the business, notably Harry Nilsson and Keith Moon, and the bash mixed some business with lots of pleasure.

In October Lennon had begun recording *Rock 'n' Roll*, an album born in court but that became a celebration of his musical origins. Not long after Lennon shared the stage with Chuck Berry on the *Mike Douglas Show*, his publisher filed a lawsuit claiming that "Come Together" sounded a little too similar to Berry's "You Can't Catch Me," even including the shared lyric, "Here come old flat-top." The case reached New York courts in 1973, and ended when Lennon agreed to record "You Can't Catch Me" on his next album.

However unfortunate the motivation, the timing was right for Lennon to take a break from writing songs of cutting-edge importance and simply enjoy playing old-time rock and roll.

"I had enough of trying to be deep," Lennon recalled of his ambitions.[19] "Why can't I have some fun? When I wasn't singing my own deep personal thoughts, it was to sing rock 'n' roll, which is what I started with."

Jukebox nuggets from those sessions included "Peggy Sue," a take on Little Richard's "Slippin' and Slidin'" that confirmed

Lennon as one of the great singers of straight-out rock and roll, "Be Bop a Lula," "Ain't that a Shame," "Sweet Little Sixteen," and what became the album's best-known track, "Stand By Me," which was stamped with Lennon's distinctive signature on the Drifters' classic. (The eventual release of *Rock 'n' Roll* was a story in itself: Lennon deferred the producer role to Phil Spector, whose eccentricities by then were more than just quirky. Spector stormed into one recording session dressed as a surgeon and fired a gun at the acoustic tile ceiling, the report originating within inches of Lennon. "If you're gonna kill me, kill me," Lennon shouted.[20] "But don't fuck with my ears, I need 'em." Recordings made in California in late 1973 disappeared with Spector for independent production until he was sidetracked by a March 1974 auto accident. Lennon later attempted to recreate the work in New York, and dueling versions and legal claims stalled the album's release until 1975.)

Playing some simple rock and roll numbers, which was a kind of home for John, a place he could always get back to whenever he wanted, now became another long and complicated process. Outside of the studio in Southern California, Lennon's life took a drink-fueled downward spiral. The duplex-centered party was fun at first: musicians, movie stars, and former Beatles lounged poolside, bar-hopped with abandon, and gave in to their urges. It was an oddly productive time too, during which Lennon produced Nilsson's *Pussy Cats*. Ringo was around, living and enjoying a Hollywood life; the brief presence of Paul McCartney prompted the obvious speculations.

McCartney had been in Los Angeles for a few days, perhaps

prompted by the opportunity to have time with Lennon sans Yoko. While McCartney was in town, he and Linda dropped in on a March 1974 session Lennon helmed at the Record Plant in Burbank for Nilsson's *Pussy Cats*; work on that album suddenly seemed irrelevant. The room fell silent when the Beatles' coauthors were present, in the same room yet somehow separate from Nilsson, Stevie Wonder, and several seasoned studio players. As recalled in Christopher Sandford's *McCartney*, everything froze until Lennon broke the tension.[21]

"Valiant Paul McCartney, I presume?" Lennon greeted his old partner, the name pulled from a Christmas play the boys had performed on British radio so very long ago.

"Sir Jasper Lennon, I presume?" McCartney responded on cue. They shook hands, a warm but subdued atmosphere enhanced by the attentions on them.

"There were fifty other people playing," Lennon exaggerated later when he recalled that night in an interview. "But they were all just watching me and Paul."[22]

They jammed to a few oldies with Paul on drums and Lennon on guitar, as always returning to the familiar ground they shared as teenagers—before the Beatles, screaming fans, triumphs and tragedies, wives, and endless lawsuits. They hadn't broken up because of the music. They ripped through "Lucille," "Cupid," something called "Bluesy Jam," and two takes of "Stand by Me." Tapes of the impromptu performance resurfaced years later as a bootleg product entitled "A Toot and a Snore in '74," the title a reference to an overheard offer of cocaine. The product was not something they would have released, scattered bits and pieces of songs pulled from strained memories amid the unspoken expectations. It was fun, but the time and place weren't fated for anything further.

Pang captured a few photographs of the former partners seated on patio furniture, hands shielding their eyes from the bright California sun. They appeared relaxed in this casual moment away from the public's expectations. Paul later admitted he was among the first to realize that Lennon may have needed a true friend.

•　　•　　•

FOR LENNON, THE party spun out of control. He had approached the perceived freedom of being away from Yoko with gusto, but the over-the-top antics eventually dragged him into an abyss. "It was a madhouse," he later said. "I realized I was in charge, I wasn't just one of the boys. A company was expecting me to produce this record out of a gang of drunken lunatics."[23]

The lost weekend faded in time and Lennon returned to New York—although not immediately to Yoko—and in the summer of 1974 recorded *Walls and Bridges*, what would be his last collection of new material for six years. Back in the Record Plant, Lennon passed on the gun-toting Spector and produced the sessions himself, the songs inspired by his separation from Yoko and downward spiral in California.

Lennon missed Yoko, perhaps the other Beatles. He would later describe on the BBC's *Old Grey Whistle Test* a situation not of peer pressure but peer acceptance: that Nilsson, Keith Moon, and company weren't going to keep Lennon's behavior in check.

"I usually have somebody there who says, 'Okay Lennon. Shut up,'" he remarked, whether referring to Yoko, former wives, or fellow Beatles. "But I didn't have anybody round me to say 'Shut up,' and I just went on and on."

Recovering from a lengthy hangover in many ways, in "Nobody Loves You (When You're Down and Out)" Lennon recalled a bad night of drinking, a legendary romp when he was bounced out of the Troubadour club in LA, a three a.m. bar-worthy confession of self-pity. He wondered in lyric where his true friends, his own peace, might be found.

"Nobody loves you when you're down and out," Lennon sang. Instead of reliving his youth, his recent antics had him feeling his age: "Nobody loves you when you're old and gray . . . I've shown you everything, I've got nothing to hide."

Lennon told the tale himself through song of the fallen idol response: "Everybody loves you when you're six foot in the ground."

•   •   •

TIRED OF WAITING, John Lennon took the offensive.

There had been limited progress with immigration during Lennon's California blowout. In early 1974 Leon Wildes had finalized "nonpriority status" for Lennon, which allowed them time to properly address the many remaining questions through the system.

"I requested documentation relating to the nonpriority

program," Wildes says, "a humanitarian program that was not part of the statute or regulations and simply a matter of secret law." Wildes documented numerous cases where, due to hardship or family obligations, "aliens who were fully deportable—including those with multiple convictions for serious drug offenses, murder, and rape—were nevertheless permitted to remain in this country."

Wildes sensed some encouragement when he was able to convince the federal prosecutors to publish the complaint. "The US attorney said it had to be published, even though it was against his client," Wildes says. "They have limited capacity to remove aliens and they should only be removing the serious aliens, not disrupting lives. It was later called 'deferred departure.' He ordered that the Lennon case should be considered, and nobody would touch the case before."

Wildes fought long and hard to get his hands on the documents and memos that told the tale of the true motivations behind the deportation attempt, dating back to Strom Thurmond's cover letter advising that deportation would be a good "strategy countermeasure." A paper trail began to emerge, and Wildes soon reviewed files including the Senate Internal Security Committee report that attempted to link Lennon to plans for disrupting the Republican convention.

Wildes returned to court in October 1974 with a judicial challenge: it was the government, not the rock singer, that had crossed legal lines. Given the developments of the Watergate investigation that resulted in the unprecedented August 1974 resignation of a president, Lennon's paranoia suddenly didn't seem as far-fetched.

The affidavit submitted in Lennon's name to Judge Fieldsteel launched a counterattack, an accusation that a few years earlier might have seemed the product of ego but made far more sense given the current state of political affairs. Lennon had been "selectively prosecuted in a discriminatory manner," the affidavit began: "I have been the subject of illegal surveillance activities on the part of the government; as a result, my case and the various applications filed in my behalf have been prejudged for reasons unrelated to my immigration status."[24]

•   •   •

LENNON MAY NOT have known he was about to take an extended bow.

If falling short of the sales success achieved by other Beatles bothered Lennon, the *Walls and Bridges* album reached the top of the album charts, aided by the number one hit duet with Elton John, "Whatever Gets You Through the Night."

When they had recorded the song in July, Elton John made a bold studio declaration that the single would top the charts, which Lennon doubted. A bet was made, and Lennon "paid up" by returning to Madison Square Garden as surprise guest during an October 28, 1974, Elton John show. The hit duet was joined by renditions of "I Saw Her Standing There" and "Lucy in the Sky with Diamonds," which Elton had recorded that year as a tribute.

Lennon walked offstage to find Yoko waiting in the wings, as orchestrated by Elton John, who had become friend to both that year. The public was unaware of backstage, private conversations among friends who—no matter the harsh opinions aired about Yoko—knew that the couple belonged together. Paul McCartney's West Coast time included more than a few heart-to-hearts on the topic, brotherly chats that had nothing to do with Beatles or rock and roll. It was time for the two to talk, to start over if possible.

"It was a great high night," Lennon told *Rolling Stone*. "A really high night. Yoko and I met backstage. I didn't know she was there, 'cause I'd have been too nervous to go on, you know. There was just that moment when we saw each other and like, it's like the movies, when time stands still? So it was a great night."[25]

The reunion proved permanent. One final issue was left to settle, a matter of principle absent any concerns of fame or fortune.

• • •

THERE WERE SOME concerns over bad publicity generated by the lost weekend, and Lennon had accepted a few invitations to portray himself in a positive light: Lennon and Harry Nilsson had made a walk-on, nonperforming appearance at a Central Park March of Dimes benefit concert in April 1974, and in May he spent two days in Philadelphia for radio appearances during WFIL-FM's "Helping Hands" marathon fundraiser before turning his attentions to *Walls and Bridges*. Approaching fall and winter, nearly three years after the INS first filed an order with the name *John Lennon* on it, Lennon took his turn at the legal plate and submitted a lawsuit: a basic First Amendment issue in which the rock star took on two former attorney generals of the United States.

As reported in a *Rolling Stone* article, "Justice for a Beatle," Wildes filed a case against the INS and former AGs John Mitchell and Richard Kleindienst, charging that "selective prosecution" was born of political motivations, and that the information used in making that case was obtained illegally through unwarranted surveillance and wiretaps. The lawsuit simply asked US District Court Judge Richard Owen to let Lennon prove the claim, and Wildes did just that.

Litigation, especially when involving a government agency, can take time; the months crawled by, and Lennon's priority turned to his marriage more than his career. Patiently, Lennon's legal case grew with each new piece of discovery. As with Watergate coming to a head, insiders came forward with damning information as INS and FBI documents were revealed. A June 1975 United Press International story explained that Wildes had the documentation to prove the deportation attempt came from Washington, and that the INS had misled the press: New York INS director Sol Marks had previously said that he made the decision on his own to proceed against Lennon; in 1975 a different story was told: "Marks said in a deposition last week he acted as a 'conduit' for instructions from Washington, which he understood to mean that 'We were not to give this man a break.'"[26]

Wildes never thought they would beat the INS on this one; the odds were too long, the deck stacked too high against Lennon. As far as the INS was concerned, Lennon's appeal was rejected and on July 17, 1975, he was again ordered to leave the country within sixty days.

On the other hand, things had changed. The lawsuit filed by

Lennon remained undecided, other voices still to be heard.

Four years after their initial introduction, Wildes was now among the Lennons' closest friends in New York. It was, then, more than just a professional pleasure when he placed an October phone call with the latest and final report on the matter: "You remember I told you we're probably not going to win this case," Wildes asked Lennon, "but that we might survive long enough for the law to be changed? I'm now calling to tell you we actually won it."

On October 7, 1975, the US Court of Appeals overturned Lennon's deportation order, confirming that the allegations made regarding the Nixon administration's role were all true.

Wildes called while Lennon was heading to the hospital, where Yoko was expected to give birth at any moment. On John Lennon's thirty-fifth birthday, October 9, 1975, so soon after hearing that their protracted fight for free speech had ended in victory, John and Yoko welcomed their son, Sean Ono Lennon.

Lennon was finally granted permanent residency in July 1976. (Asked if he harbored ill will toward Mitchell, Nixon, Thurmond, et al., Lennon shrugged and smiled at the reporters present: "Well, time wounds all heels.")

After more than a decade of fame, wealth, adulation, and the grandest trappings of sex, drugs, and rock and roll, John Lennon was—finally—a happy man.

"WE ALL SHINE ON . . ."

"Life is what happens to you while you're busy making other plans."
—JOHN LENNON, "Beautiful Boy"

I RECENTLY WATCHED John Lennon's performance of "Mother" at the One-to-One concert. Forty years have passed since the Madison Square Garden concert. The show was captured on film, transferred to videotape at some point, and eventually digitized. I've seen it countless times. Tens of thousands of people were in the arena, but Lennon made you feel there was, in fact, a one-to-one connection between artist and listener. He had a way of doing that, of singing simple truths, addressing his lyrics to "my friends" and making it believable.

"You were seeing him the way a lot of people saw him," Tex Gabriel told me, adding that during the actual performance Tex was too focused on his job—and perhaps a bit too young—to fully appreciate the moment. That came later.

Lennon is remembered by his fellow musicians as basically a good, decent guy. He was no saint, nor did he claim to be. He had a temper, one that sometimes flared up when he was trying to record a piece of music. He also apologized when he did lose his cool. If they'd wanted to, the Elephants, Bob Gruen, and Lennon's other close friends had opportunities to tell tales about the sinner behind the martyred idol; they haven't because—unlike those in search of Lennon's dark side—they actually knew the man.

In many ways we all did. People know where they were on that night in December 1980 the way we recall tragedies we simply don't understand, like the assassination of a president or terrorist attacks on a nation. I was too young for Beatlemania, but my generation—and those that followed—discovered the lads as we did other hot bands. They were better than most—if not all—of the newer musical acts. The Beatles' music felt fresh, original, and filled with mysteries. Still does.

I was in suburban Detroit the night Lennon was killed, no longer a teenager and less than six months away from leaving my parents' house. A picture of Lennon hung on my bedroom wall: one of four portraits packaged with the "White Album." Somewhere around the time of *Sgt. Pepper*, album covers had become works of pop art with enough space—compared to a CD case or the nonexistent cover of a download—for images bizarre or beautiful; for lyrics printed large enough to read (or be read into);

for cardboard sleeves to contain posters and other goodies. (Hall of fame honors to Cheech & Chong's comedy album *Big Bambú*, which included an enormous rolling paper worthy of a joint large enough to challenge John Sinclair.)

We realized right away that night just how much we'd miss Lennon. The mythology around John Lennon grew over the years. He was not always known back then for the same things he is known for today. He was the "weird one" of the Beatles, the one who lost his mind to a woman and walked away from rock-and-roll fame to raise his kid: that wasn't really considered cool back then.

What qualifies as "cool" changes from year to year. Lennon's core principles didn't: nonviolent, constructive activism was a constant, as was his opinion that love was better than hate, peace better than war. Maybe we've changed. A lot of people who thought they were right back in 1972 turned out to be wrong.

Some things take a little longer to understand.

•   •   •

WAYNE GABRIEL WAS far too young, he later realized, to appreciate the preciousness of his time with John Lennon: no one knew back then that Elephant's Memory would be the last regular band to work with Lennon.

The association with Lennon opened doors, including the introduction to Chuck Berry, whose 1973 album *Bio* featured a rare guest instrumental: "I'm the only other guitar player he ever let solo on an album," Gabriel says.

Gabriel saw Lennon a final time in the fall of 1980, an

accidental encounter outside of the Dakota, two New Yorkers looking for a cab or late for an appointment. A shame, they agreed, that their musical journey a decade earlier came to an abrupt end.

"I went to New York to make it," Gabriel says. "When I got with John Lennon that dream came true. Where could it go from there? Things didn't work out the way I envisioned."

They rarely do, I point out.

"No, they never do," Gabriel sighs.

•   •   •

OUR TALKS WERE somewhat frustrating from a reporter's perspective: the conversations were too enjoyable and we often drifted to matters irrelevant to the story but far more important—family, friends, memories of common ground in New York or Detroit. We ended our last session with words and thoughts similar to what Lennon had said at the Madison Square Garden closing: *no sweat, we'll get it right next time.*

Like too many other things, that time never came. Early in 2010 Wayne "Tex" Gabriel was diagnosed with Creutzfeldt-Jakob syndrome, a degenerative disorder that took his life in May of the same year. He left behind a loving wife, Marisa LaTorre, children Ataia and Savion Gabriel from his first marriage to Sandra Fulton, stepchildren Sarah and David Goldfarb, and friends who miss him for reasons having nothing to do with guitar chords.

•   •   •

JOHN SINCLAIR NEVER compromised his values, a qualified admission.

"I never sold out," Sinclair says. "Nobody ever offered me anything."

These days, an active Sinclair is as likely to be seen in the jazz clubs of New Orleans as he is in Detroit or Amsterdam, though he does get his share of questions about the good ol' days of hippie revolution. Sinclair knows it sounds old-fashioned to look back with a sense of loss, but the world has changed considerably.

"We've got a void," Sinclair says. "There will never be another Beatles. That's why John Lennon and Yoko Ono were so important: they could reach the masses of people because of who he was. The billboards in Times Square, the bed-ins for peace: all that stuff was powerful because it rang everybody's bell."

Sinclair says that Lennon's speech at the Crisler Arena about apathetic youth was more prophetic than anything, and holds true today.

"It was a call to action," Sinclair says. "They don't make singles like 'Give Peace a Chance' anymore. They don't see the idea of developing something over a period of time. They want it to happen within the next news cycle."

The Movement, Sinclair says, resurfaced in many ways with Occupy Wall Street, the Arab Spring, and revolutions launched online in similar spirit.

"We needed that," Sinclair says. "If they're lucky they'll make it last. This is the best thing to happen to these kids. Who wants to just be a consumer? No matter how many groovy products they got, how many iPads can you have?"

•   •   •

WHETHER JOHN LENNON "abandoned" the Movement out of self-preservation was a question for some; Rennie Davis thought so at the time. No grudges, of course; true activists always found different ways to protest.

"The thing that was cool about John was a quality I saw in many people who were deeply committed to the Movement," Davis says. "People might disagree about tactics and approaches, but there is a deep level of commitment. That's what I saw in John. He was the real deal; he really believed in what we were trying to do."

Time mellows people in different ways. Davis was among those who sought new paths to similar goals. Meditation caught his fancy, one of many doors that Lennon and the Beatles opened for a generation. "People began talking about changing ourselves," Davis says. "You'd be amazed how many people said yes to that."

Davis did, becoming in 1973 an acolyte of Guru Maharaj Ji, the sixteen-year-old leader of the Divine Light Mission, which hosted a three-day meditation bash at the Houston Astrodome. World peace, they said, began with inner peace.

"John talked to me about it," Davis says. "'If you wanna change the world, Rennie, you've got to change yourself.'"

Davis says he's had ample time to think about those days, to reconsider positions taken forty years earlier.

"When I look back at that time, I lean a little more toward saying that John may have been right," Davis says. "The real thing that's going on here is, we've got to change ourselves in order to change the outside world."

•   •   •

GARY VAN SCYOC thought he had one more chance to join John Lennon on tour, a conversation that hinted at renewed professional opportunities. After Elephant's Memory dissolved, Van Scyoc continued a studio career behind Neil Sedaka, Paul Simon, Chuck Berry, and other artists, and in 2012 he and Adam Ippolito joined Birds of Paradox, a band that included Steve Holley and Laurence Juber, one-time members of Paul McCartney's Wings. "Real incestuous," Van Scyoc laughs at the Beatles connections.

Van Scyoc last spoke with Lennon in 1980 when he called to tell him about some new material he'd been working on. "John and I had no problems," Van Scyoc said. "No airs between us. He loved my material and was very nice about it."

Lennon was nearing the end of recording *Double Fantasy*, and told Van Scyoc he was planning a tour—again—and there might be room for another bassist. "He wasn't sure; said maybe, possibly I could do it, but nothing ever came of that."

Instead, Van Scyoc recalls the night of December 8; he and a friend were at a jazz club on the Upper West Side, "right across the street from the Dakota," Van Scyoc says. "The set ended at eleven p.m., and we hit the street no more than five minutes after. There were two police cars with their lights on. I looked at my friend and said, 'Oh my God, something happened to John.' I don't know why I knew that; but then, why was I chosen to play with a Beatle?"

Van Scyoc knew Lennon in ways the thousands of people that crowded around the corner of Seventy-Second Street and Central Park West didn't, but they knew him just the same.

"There were so many people there," Van Scyoc says. "It was just unbelievable the way the crowd grew; thousands of people were there within hours."

•   •   •

JERRY RUBIN, ONCE called out by a group of fellow activists and hippies for "b.o. and other hygiene habits," followed the fashions of the so-called "Me Decade" 1970s, embracing movements such as EST, meditation, acupuncture, bioenergetics, and holistic therapies. A hit with the late-1970s Studio 54 cocaine-and-disco crowd, Rubin embraced competitive capitalism in 1980 and became a stockbroker with Wall Street's John Muir & Co. By the early 1990s, Rubin was soaking in Southern California sunshine and selling a powdered drink mix; the company was hit with a 1992 class action lawsuit as a pyramid scheme.

Rubin died in November 1994 when he was hit by a car while jaywalking in Hollywood. Fellow Chicago Seven alum Tom Hayden told the *Los Angeles Times* Rubin was "a great life force," adding, "his willingness to defy authority for constructive purposes will be missed. Up to the end he was defying authority."

•   •   •

OLD HIPPIES DON'T always fade away, and many took the skills they learned in the Movement and applied them in other ways when the Movement subsided. Tariq Ali applied the same passion that published *Red Mole* into his work as an author, filmmaker, historian, and novelist—never surrendering the activist title or role in life.

John Lennon didn't shy away from the revolution, Ali points out, and all evidence indicates that his views would remain consistent over time.

"He did back off from some of those people," Ali says of Lennon distancing himself from Rubin and the Yippies. "But I don't think he backed off politically. I have absolutely no doubt that had he been with us he would have been against the Iraq war. Even Mick Jagger wrote songs about the Iraq war."

When discussing the explosive topics of the late 1960s and early 1970s, Ali still gets "lots of questions all over the world about that period, and especially about John Lennon." Some of the songs are still put forth in the same manner as in 1972, Ali says, recalling an Occupy protest where the crowd sang "Power to the People."

"So certain things remain. They don't have the same impact that they did in the sixties and seventies," Ali says. "But they remain as extremely important echoes in the world in which we live."

•   •   •

ADAM IPPOLITO NEVER saw John Lennon again, although he had encounters both pleasant and not so warm with Yoko Ono. Ippolito returned to California in the late 1970s for recording and performance work including the Joffrey Ballet and joining the disco-funk Kool and the Gang ("Celebration").

In 1986 Capitol Records and Yoko Ono Lennon released the One-to-One concert, *John Lennon Live in New York City*, portions of which were included in a 1988 documentary, *Imagine: John Lennon.*

Ippolito was in a difficult position. His keyboard work at Madison Square Garden seemed at times to be matched with video of Yoko seated at a piano. Elephant's Memory as a whole filed suit—Ippolito was lead plaintiff—that the video made unauthorized use of their names and images, and that Yoko "only pretended to" play. There were disagreements over which of the two performances was used for the audio tracks and video images. As described by the *New York Law Journal*, "the credit given Ono Lennon constituted a 'palming off' of Ippolito's performance." The individual case, however, had no legal backing: the original concert credits simply listed musicians and instruments played, including Yoko on keyboard; specific songs were not identified.

The video itself also faced new arguments about technology and copyright. New York trial court Judge Harold Baer Jr. said the band members were correct: consent to the use of their names for the 1972 show and original broadcast on television did not mean permission was given "to all uses for all time." Future sales of the VHS edition of the show were halted, although it would be frequently aired on nonprofit public television. Images of the band and their performance in the broader *Imagine* documentary were, at best, "visual footnotes."

Time passed and memories faded. Ippolito says that he and his wife met Yoko backstage at a New York event, long after the lawsuit and decades after the crazy year when they shared a roller-coaster ride of rock and revolution. It was nice, Ippolito says, old friends catching up on the things that really matter. The strength of peaceful, loving memories far outlasted any momentary disputes.

Ippolito subsequently played on more successful "hit" records than he did with Lennon, and before larger audiences, but those seem like just another day at the office compared to their time together.

"I've played bigger venues," Ippolito says, "but [playing with John Lennon] was the biggest gig of my life, I would have to say."

•   •   •

DAVID PEEL DEFINED "underground legend" as the New York hippie who said the pope smoked pot and—for a brief, shining moment—his association with John Lennon. Arguably one of pop culture's most famous footnotes, Peel took his guitar to New York's Zuccotti Park in April 2012 and joined an Occupy Wall Street encampment.

The *New York Times* took note that, at sixty-eight, Peel "still has his guitar, his three chords, and his festive, irreverent marijuana shout-music." The kids likely didn't know the legend of Peel, but one Village "old-timer" perked up at the name: "The marijuana song, right?"

The *Times* piece was a sad bit of nostalgia. Peel did compose a ditty called "Up Against the Wall Street" for a stab at relevance, yet he seemed resigned to his legacy, having once been featured in Lennon's place on an FBI poster. Peel still, the *Times* said, wears Lennon-style sunglasses, lives in the same Avenue B apartment, and "survives on modest royalties, small gig fees and the sale of old and current records."

The *Times* reminded people that Lennon was quoted as saying that Peel "writes beautiful songs," in spite of criticism that Peel "can't sing, or he really can't play."

•   •   •

MORE THAN A dozen players came and went since Stan Bronstein and Rick Frank—who met while providing the music in Manhattan strip clubs—formed Elephant's Memory. Only a few albums carried the band's name during their run; a final LP, *Our Island Music*, was credited to Stan Bronstein and the Elephant's Memory Band. The "island" was Manhattan, which remained their home long after parting ways with John Lennon. Bronstein recorded a final record, *Living on the Avenue*, in 1976, and continued work as a studio player on both saxophone and clarinet. Frank passed away in 2003.

In 2011, Bronstein battled lung and brain cancer. The Sweet Relief Musician's Fund rallied to help, a cause quickly embraced by Yoko, who recalled Bronstein as "a passionate and uniquely talented musician . . . he is also good hearted and makes his band follow his lead with spirit of fun and joy. His reliable presence affected the performance of both John and I as well. We both loved and respected him."

In August 2012 Bronstein was inducted into the New York Blues Hall of Fame at Kenny's Castaways, a Bleecker Street staple since 1967 that closed after forty-five years.

•   •   •

IN HIS BOOK *I'll Be Right Back*, talk show host Mike Douglas recalled the network panic at the thought of Jerry Rubin—let alone a card-carrying Black Panther—being broadcast to millions of housewives.

"Rather than regret what happened, I appreciate it," Douglas wrote. "It was great confrontational television, a harsh exchange of ideas. But there were no chairs thrown, no noses broken, not a single word bleeped out. It was emotional but not offensive, with the added bonus of allowing people to see what a genuinely nice fellow John Lennon was."

Douglas said Lennon had promised to revisit the program, and when word got out that he was recording again in 1980, Douglas invited Lennon to join him for a week. Work on *Double Fantasy* took longer than expected, and Douglas accepted Lennon's request to postpone the appearance, which had been planned for early December: "I can recall the exact moment when a grim staffer gave me the tragic news that John Lennon had been shot and killed. It was the day of his scheduled appearance. There was no sense to be made of it. All I know is, we lost one of the most creative forces in music that day, and an exceptional man."

•   •   •

PEACE CORPS DIRECTOR Joseph Blatchford—"one leg in each generation"—had mixed feelings about his former boss, but was all too familiar with the attitudes of Nixon's inner circle. Protests were considered not just unpatriotic but dangerous; Martin Luther King was equated with the riots of Detroit or

Watts. Fundamental ideas protected under the US constitution attracted suspicions.

"The peace symbol mainly stood for the war in Vietnam," Blatchford says. "It was a symbol of the antiwar movement, and it was considered very divisive."

Blatchford was surprised he didn't see more of that spirit forty years later when America was again engaged in conflict. Perhaps, Blatchford says, because there was no draft for the wars in Iraq and Afghanistan there wasn't the same spark as in the 1960s. There were some protests, though, and Blatchford took note of those standing for peace.

"I was in San Francisco when the war began, and there was a gathering of a lot of people," Blatchford says. "They all had gray hair: I think I remembered a couple of them from the Berkeley riots."

Saying "peace" in wartime—then and now—can be viewed as sincere hope or treason. Lennon, Blatchford says, saw it as more than just a slogan.

"I think with him it was broader than that. All I remember is the wonderful music and his songwriting," Blatchford says. "I don't remember anything about the radicalism. He and his wife were very idealistic in their desires for peace. I don't think it was antiestablishment in his mouth, I think it was genuinely ... peace. You know? Lennon, to me, is connected more with a desire for peace and hands across the sea and goodwill and that kind of thing as opposed to the internal divisions within our own society over the war."

•   •   •

ATTORNEY LEON WILDES never again claimed to be unfamiliar with John Lennon; the legal challenge they waged together remained a personal and professional highlight. An expert in immigration law, Wildes teaches at the Benjamin N. Cardozo School of Law, lectures, and has testified before Congress on the subject. Besides being among a handful of New Yorkers to call John and Yoko true friends, Wildes says their court battle was, in its own way, as influential as Lennon's artistic achievements.

"There were a number of significant legal accomplishments in that case," Wildes says, having penned five *Law Review* articles on the subject, three of which dealt with the nonpriority provision. "Today that's the hottest item in immigration law," Wildes says.

In hindsight, Wildes notes that the FBI's often inept "investigation" of Lennon indicated that it really was a low-priority matter. It's impossible to believe that any agent worth a badge couldn't find a photo of John Lennon.

"I don't think they assigned their top people," Wildes says. "Maybe they just didn't take people off important investigations to follow these artists around for political reasons. Some of the people assigned to the case were probably second rate."

It wasn't, however, a laughing matter at the time. Wildes said that Nixon and his administration considered dissidents and immigrants equally as enemies of the state.

"Nixon took off after illegal aliens," Wildes says. "He was running a kind of Mafia operation. He assumed that if the president did it, it must be legal, but he knew damn well it couldn't be legal."

Wildes has his own wistful wish that Lennon were still with

us today; his voice on immigration would be welcome in the twenty-first century.

"Lennon would have been outraged by the treatment of illegal aliens and how they're used as political footballs," Wildes says. "The press would have eaten it up. Lennon had a way of expressing himself that appealed to the way the average person feels about unfairness in the system. John was brilliant. It's a tragedy that we don't have him around to speak up respectfully against the injustices of immigration law or the way's it's carried out. He had that gift."

●   ●   ●

CIGARETTE MANUFACTURER PHILLIP Morris introduced its Virginia Slims brand in 1968 to a target audience of young, professional women who considered themselves "liberated" while they smoked. The catch phrase was: *You've come a long way, baby.* The slogan was featured in print ads and television commercials; cigarettes were advertised on TV until 1971, something that surprises younger people today as much as the idea of a sexist marketing campaign designed to attract feminists.

The women's movement has come a long way, Gloria Steinem says, in spite of the bias of commercial marketing. It just took a while.

"From a historical point of view, the suffragist and abolitionist movements gained for women of all races and black men a legal identity as human beings," Steinem says. "Before suffrage and abolition it was possible to own women and to own black men, literally, as objects."

Steinem recalls Lennon for reasons separate from music. Years before it was en vogue for men to accept the role of "house husband" or embrace raising a baby, Steinem says Lennon had what it took. He never did worry about the masculinity of appreciating art or respectfully deferring to his wife. Lennon wrote about it in *Skywriting by Word of Mouth*, a collection of essays from his "retirement" years. When the press described him as a recluse who would never "work again," Lennon posed a question long asked by women: "If bringing up a child isn't work, what is?"

Lennon defied gender conventions as easily as he did musical inspirations and racial attitudes. "He had an equal partnership with Yoko," Steinem says. "The fact that he stayed home to raise his son and was a real parent had a huge impact, almost as much impact as his songs."

•   •   •

IT'S NOT AN urban legend: Richard Nixon had an "enemies list" that documented the presidential paranoia. Lennon's name was included, and not as "favorite Beatle."

Making the list was easy for Ron Dellums: all thirteen founders of the Congressional Black Caucus were included.

"I wore that like a badge," Dellums notes. He says the bottom line was "this incredible force of national security apparatus overreacting to people who were expressing their legitimate rights to organize, assemble, and express themselves."

Dellums retained his congressional seat until 1998. In the twenty-first century Dellums served two terms as mayor of

Oakland, California, and says that in spite of the advancements made, some still needed to learn the lessons of the era. In 2007 tensions rose after a Bay Area Rapid Transit officer shot and killed a young African American. The officer was put on trial. Awaiting the verdict, Dellums says he was approached by a young man planning a vigil of sorts. Dellums was asked to join the crowd to confirm, he was told, "their right to be there." The young man indicated that his group would not be allowed to hold a vigil without the mayor's presence.

They didn't need him for that, Dellums pointed out, but perhaps a recent-history lesson was in order.

"I told them we fought that fight fifty years ago," Dellums says. "If you need someone to validate your right to be at Fourteenth and Broadway, then we wasted fifty years."

As long as they did it peacefully: violent civil conflicts—whether bomb-throwing dissidents or soldiers and cops shooting at will—had been tried: "We don't have to reinvent the barricades; we did that. People died in that. You wanna run around in a ski mask lighting up a car? Come on, man. We went down that road."

Dellums's message remained consistent as a community activist, congressman, and big-city mayor. The core values, he says, were staying true to a cause and getting involved.

"I think John Lennon was faithful," Dellums says. "He showed up for the fight."

Those who shared the battles of the sixties, the civil rights, antiwar, and pro–social justice battles, have been proven to be on the right side of most issues over time.

"We were exonerated by history," Dellums reflects. "Our generation, that time in America, we changed things. Are there struggles that need to be waged and principals to be embraced? Absolutely yes. We did change the world, but we didn't make it perfect."

•   •   •

THE MOVEMENT WASN'T dead after Nixon's reelection, Paul Krassner says, it simply evolved. Krassner too sees parallels between the sixties protests and twenty-first-century developments like Occupy and the Arab Spring; he admits he was surprised that the Internet and social media evolved into a forum for those very movements: "I'm old enough to remember when media was a plural noun and somehow became singular. I make fun of Facebook and YouTube—you can spend all day watching cats play the piano and never see the same cat twice—but they have changed the world in the sense of communicating a revolution from different countries, influencing them."

Ever the realist, Krassner expresses amusement at the accidental nature of how social networks became a forum for online revolution. "It's not something [Mark] Zuckerberg thought of," Krassner says. "He thought it was a way to meet girls. It's encouraging to see how young people get their information from social networks rather than the mainstream media. Or maybe they're just allergic to paper."

Taking a lesson from the era, Krassner points out that "the spirit lived on," and the issues outlived the fashions. Krassner says that Lennon was an inspiration, more than willing to try new ideas and embrace different causes: he also knew that there was a limit to what pop culture heroes could do.

"I think he was very savvy," Krassner says. "It seemed naïve to think it would make a difference if he and Yoko got in bed in Canada to end the war. I don't know if he was taken advantage of; everybody wanted something from him. They consciously made the decision to use their celebrity to make a better world."

•   •   •

WE KNOW WHAT happened to John Lennon, as we felt we knew the man himself. Forty-plus years after the Beatles ended their run, three and a half decades after a senseless murder, there remains a desire to revisit that friendship. Maybe we're trying to get to know ourselves a little better, our generation(s), and just what the hell happened back then.

John Lennon's years of revolution were born in the sixties and took a rowdy ride deep into the 1970s. There was, he said, a price to pay for doing what he believed, a cost that couldn't be covered even by the resources of a millionaire rock star. John and Yoko's search for Kyoko Cox remained an unfinished quest long after his death—Lennon never did see his wife reunited with her daughter. Tony Cox successfully kept the girl from Yoko in spite of the Texas court rulings: months became years, the girl became an adult. But family ties are strong, and in 1997 Kyoko Cox reached out for a reunion so that Yoko could meet her granddaughter, Emi, and not for the last time.

John and Yoko remained true New Yorkers until his death and found, against so many odds, inner peace and perspective on the past. Such things take time, Lennon knew.

"People said the Beatles were the Movement, but we were only part of the Movement," Lennon said. With the same idea shared by kindred souls throughout history who had "leadership" thrust upon them, Lennon said—as he told Rennie Davis about finding peace within yourself—that looking elsewhere for answers doesn't work: "Leaders and father figures are the mistake of all the generations before us. All of us rely on Nixon or Jesus or whoever we rely on; it's a lack of responsibility that you expect somebody else to do it. I won't be a leader. Everybody is a leader. People thought the Beatles were leaders, but they weren't, and now people are finding that out."

Actually, they were, only not in the way they might have thought. Rarely a day goes by without encountering a reference to the Beatles or John Lennon; a song, an idea, a message bearing their image.

The spirit of John Lennon long outlived the decade, inspiring thoughts of peace, activism, honesty, and the best traits of kinder, gentler hippie-dom. At the closing ceremonies of the 2012 Olympics in London, audiences were stunned, many moved to tears, by a video performance of Lennon singing "Imagine."

His life and music still inspire, and so does his senseless death. In March 2013, on what would have been their anniversary, Yoko Ono tweeted a photo of Lennon's blood-stained glasses with a note as to how many Americans have been killed by gun violence since that terrible December day. President Barack Obama retweeted the posting.

The tragedy was understood immediately, the legacy needed a little time. Maybe it takes longer to recognize peace, as a global wish or inside ourselves. First you have to imagine it's possible.

ACKNOWLEDGMENTS

*"Thank you on behalf of the
group and ourselves."*

WAYNE "TEX" GABRIEL and I only spoke a few times before his diagnosis in March 2010. The project continued as he'd hoped it would, with encouragement and support from Marisa LaTorre, Bob Prewitt, Gary Van Scyoc, and Adam Ippolito. Thanks also to my agent, Eric Myers of the Spieler Agency. No better home for this exists than Seven Stories Press and I thank Sophia Ioannou for seeing the story first. Editors Veronica Liu, Gabe Espinal, and Jesse Lichtenstein helped shepherd the project, and publisher Dan Simon went above and beyond as he patiently turned a reporter into a storyteller. The pictorial section of this book is as much the creation of Silvia Stramenga and Stewart Cauley as the talented photographers on display.

No island, this man: I humbly note the encouragement through a decidedly bumpy road from friends and family in their own way: Phil Allmen, Naresh Gunaratnam ("M. D."), Bruce Goldberg, Cheryl Huckins, Lynn Helland, Lindsey Kingston (go get 'em, Tiger), and Tamra Ward (Dear Lady).

My father, Eldon Mitchell, would have smiled in spite of himself. My mother, Ruby Mitchell, was able to know we made it this far, and always knew we would. Glad the journey included my Marine Corps–worthy son, Alex. This journey and all else I share with Linda Remilong, my longtime co-passenger, together for the long ride. The trip was well celebrated in family toasts with her daughters, beautiful bride Jenny and her equally gorgeous sister, Lisa. If I weren't lucky enough, my favorite four-legged fur-balls were always nearby while I was typing: Josie—too cute for words—and Abbey (yes, as in "Road"). There were doubts, of course, but like the man said: "There's nothing you can do that can't be done."

AUTHOR'S NOTE: SOURCES AND METHODOLOGY

THE FOUNDATION OF this story was built on my interviews with Elephant's Memory bandsmen Wayne "Tex" Gabriel, Gary Van Scyoc, and Adam Ippolito. Theirs was a perspective, supported by newspaper and magazine accounts, which chronicles Lennon the musician during an often-overlooked yet productive period of recording and performing.

Lennon's associations with prominent activists of the day were the subject of my conversations with Tariq Ali, John Sinclair, Rennie Davis, Leni Sinclair, and Jay Craven, who provided insights beyond the voluminous FBI reports featuring their names. Lennon's ensuing legal battle was best explained by his attorney, Leon Wildes, who in turn guided me to further documents I might not have found without his help..

The issues raised by Lennon—and a generation—were not limited to opposition of a war or a president. Conversations (rather than "interviews") with feminist leader Gloria Steinem and Representative Ron Dellums provided an informed then-and-now perspective on, respectively, the women's movement and civil rights struggle. Satirist Paul Krassner and former Peace Corps director Joseph Blatchford had brief yet revealing encounters with Lennon that added immeasurably to the story.

Along with this author's interviews and conversations, research included several key published accounts to whose authors I offer due respect and gratitude, including Stu Werbin (and so many others) from *Rolling Stone*, talk-show hosts Dick Cavett and Mike Douglas, and author Jon Wiener, whose battle to make public the FBI's John Lennon documents was an admirable example of activist journalism. Along with the sources cited throughout the book, the author relied primarily on the following materials:

Chapter One was built on my conversations with Tariq Ali in January 2012, Rennie Davis in October 2011, Peter Andrews in November 2011, and time spent in Detroit with John Sinclair in October 2011 and Leni Sinclair in November 2011. Accounts of John Lennon's early days in New York were supported by Stu Werbin's 1972 *Rolling Stone* article, "John & Jerry & David & John

& Leni & Yoko," Henrik Hertzberg's "Talk of the Town" article from the *New Yorker*, and *Red Mole* interviews with Lennon by Tariq Ali and Robin Blackburn. Additional insights were found in footage by French TV reporter Jean-François Vallee, and interviews by *Apple to the Core* authors Peter McCabe and Robert Schonfeld.

Lennon's experiences with Elephant's Memory in Chapter Two were based on my talks with Bob Prewitt in January and June 2010, Gary Van Scyoc in January and May 2010 and June and September 2011, Adam Ippolito in July and September 2011, and Wayne "Tex" Gabriel in 2009 and 2010. My interviews with Rennie Davis in October 2011 and Jay Craven in November 2011 provided details on Lennon's involvement with the Yippies. Additional information was obtained from viewing Lennon's appearance on the *David Frost Show*. (Conversations with the Elephants, Davis, Craven, Ali, and Sinclairs also informed subsequent chapters.)

Chapter Three's observations on Nixon's White House were informed by my interview with Joseph Blatchford in August 2011; accounts of the Nixon-Elvis meeting were confirmed by the National Security Archive of George Washington University. Lennon's cohosting of the *Mike Douglas Show* was described in the host's memoir, *I'll Be Right Back: Memories of TV's Greatest Talk Show,* and through my viewing of the episodes. FBI documents related to the John Lennon investigation were obtained online (www.vault.fbi.gov). Another source for the FBI documents was *Gimme Some Truth* by Jon Wiener.

Lennon's legal case, first explained in Chapter Four, was recounted during my interview with Leon Wildes in November 2011. Lennon's diverse encounters included those described during my talk with A. J. Weberman in October 2011. Lennon's feminist politics were the topic of my February 2012 conversation with Gloria Steinem. Additional materials on the court case were obtained from the *New York Times*, and Jon Wiener's *Come Together: John Lennon in His Time*.

Portions of Chapter Five deal with Lennon's use of a controversial word, the definition of which framed my February 2012 talk with Ron Dellums. Lennon's appearances on *The Dick Cavett Show* were viewed, with additional observations found in Cavett's memoir, *Talk Show*. Additional materials on the court case were obtained from the *New York Times*, notably the work of law columnist Grace Lichtenstein.

The West Coast trip described in Chapter Six included Lennon's time with Paul Krassner, which he discussed when we spoke in November 2011. Additional information was obtained via WABC-TV *Eyewitness News* footage of Geraldo Rivera's interviews. Concert preparations and Rivera's investigation of Willowbrook was documented by the *Atlantic* magazine and in *Lennon Revealed* by Larry Kane. Along with my viewing of the videotape of the concert, Lennon's postshow interview with *New Musical Express* provided further insight.

Press accounts in Chapter Seven of Lennon's work with the Elephants were reported in music magazines including *Cash Box*, *Melody Maker*, *New Musical Express*, and *Billboard*, along with interviews in *Rolling Stone* and the *Village Voice*. Lennon's thoughts on the ongoing INS struggle were well covered by *Rolling Stone* in Joe Treen's article, "Justice for a Beatle." Accounts of election night were told by bandsmen and recounted in Wiener's *Come Together*. Lennon's post-Elephant's work was chronicled in the book *Lennon in America*, by Geoffrey Giuliano, and other sources including *John Lennon: One Day at a Time* by Anthony Fawcett, and *McCartney* by Christopher Sandford.

NOTES

CHAPTER 1: THE ADVENT OF THE HIPPIE MESSIAH

1. Philip Norman, *John Lennon: The Life* (New York: HarperCollins, 2008), 683.

2. John Lennon, interview by Peter McCabe and Robert Schonfeld at the St. Regis Hotel, New York City, September 5, 1971, *Tittenhurst Park* blog, http://tittenhurstlennon.blogspot.com/2009/08/john-lennon-st-regis-hotel-room.html.

3. Hendrik Hertzberg, "Talk of the Town," *New Yorker*, January 8, 1972, 28.

4. Tariq Ali and Robin Blackburn, *Red Mole*, January 1971.

5. Hunter Davies, ed., *The John Lennon Letters* (New York: Little, Brown and Company, 2012), 208.

6. Ali and Blackburn, *Red Mole*

7. Paul DeRienzo, "John Lennon, David Peel and Rock's Greatest Flattery," *Villager*, December 13, 2012.

8. Geoffrey Giuliano, *Lennon in America: 1971–1980, Based in Part on the Lost Lennon Diaries* (New York: Cooper Square Press, 2000), 35.

9. Elliot Mintz, "Elliot Mintz Interviews John Lennon," *Los Angeles Free Press*, October 15–21, 1971.

10. Stu Werbin, "John & Jerry & David & John & Leni & Yoko," *Rolling Stone*, February 17, 1972.

11. John Lennon, interview by Jean-Françoise Vallee, *Pop 2*, December 1971.

12. David A. Carson, *Grit, Noise, and Revolution* (Ann Arbor: University of Michigan Press, 2005), 113.

13. Alan Glenn, "The Day a Beatle Came to Town," *Ann Arbor Chronicle*, December 27, 2009.

14. Lennon, interview by McCabe and Schonfeld, *Tittenhurst Park*.

15. Glenn, *Ann Arbor Chronicle*.

16. Ibid.

17. *The U.S. vs. John Lennon*, directed by David Leaf and John Scheinfeld (Paramount, 2006).

18. Roy Reynolds, "15,000 Attend Sinclair Rally," *Ann Arbor News*, December 11, 1971.

19. Bill Gray, "Lennon Let His Followers Down," *Detroit News*, December 13, 1971.

CHAPTER 2: JOHN AND THE ELEPHANTS

1. John Lennon, interview by Alan Smith, *New Musical Express*, reprinted in *Hit Parader*, February 1972.

2. Ben Gerson, review of *Imagine* by John Lennon, *Rolling Stone*, October 28, 1971.

3. Editorial, "Art of Hokum?" *Syracuse Post-Standard*, September 27, 1971.

4. John Lennon and Yoko Ono, "Love Letter from Two Artists," *Syracuse Post-Standard*, October 7, 1971.

5. John Lennon, interview with David Frost, *David Frost Show*, June 1969.

6. *The U.S. vs. John Lennon.*

7. Ed McCormack, "Elephant's Memory Without the Plastic," *Rolling Stone*, August 31, 1972.

8. Toby Mamis, "Take It to the Streets," *Creem*, June 1971.

9. McCormack, *Rolling Stone.*

10. Mike Jahn, "Elephant's Memory Mixes Radicalism and a Rough Sound," *New York Times*, July 4, 1971.

11. "Talent in Action," *Billboard*, July 17, 1971.

12. McCormack, *Rolling Stone.*

13. *The David Frost Show*, broadcast January 1972.

14. Jon Wiener, *Come Together: John Lennon in His Time* (New York: Random House, 1990), 198.

15. Stu Werbin, "John & Jerry & David & John & Leni & Yoko," *Rolling Stone*, February 17, 1972.

16. Ibid.

17. Richard Nusser, "Beatle With an Elephant's Memory?" *Village Voice*, January 20, 1972.

CHAPTER 3: "DOPED WITH RELIGION AND SEX AND TV"

1. Bob Gruen, *John Lennon: The New York Years* (New York: Stewart, Tabori & Chang, 2005), 52.

2. The research in this and other FBI sections is largely based on publicly available documents from the FBI's declassified files: "John Winston Lennon," FBI Records: The Vault, http://vault.fbi.gov/john-winston-lennon. Additional contextual and background information can be found in Jon Wiener, *Gimme Some Truth: The John Lennon FBI Files* (Berkeley: University of California Press, 2000).

3. Stu Werbin, "John & Jerry & David & John & Leni & Yoko," *Rolling Stone*, February 17, 1972.

4. Transcripts and correspondence from the Nixon-Presley meeting on December 21, 1970, can be found at the National Security Archive at the George Washington University, http://www.gwu.edu/~nsarchiv/nsa/elvis/elnix.html.

5. Mike Douglas, with Thomas Kelly and Michael Heaton, *I'll Be Right Back: Memories of TV's Greatest Talk Show* (New York: Simon & Schuster, 2000), 257–262.

6. Hunter Davies, ed., *The John Lennon Letters* (New York: Little, Brown and Company, 2012).

7. Night Owl Reporter, "Here They Come Again," *New York Daily News*, February 15, 1972.

8. *Mike Douglas Show*, February 14–18, 1972.

9. Douglas, *I'll Be Right Back*.

CHAPTER 4: "A THOROUGH NUISANCE

1. "John Winston Lennon," FBI Records: The Vault, http://vault.fbi.

gov/john-winston-lennon. Additional contextual and background information can be found in Jon Wiener, *Gimme Some Truth: The John Lennon FBI Files* (Berkeley: University of California Press, 2000).

2. Philip Norman, *John Lennon: The Life* (New York: HarperCollins, 2008), 577.

3. Joe Treen, "Justice for a Beatle: The Illegal Plot to Prosecute and Oust John Lennon," *Rolling Stone*, December 5, 1974.

4. Peter McCabe, "Some Sour Notes from the Bangladesh Concert," *New York*, February 28, 1972.

5. Jon Wiener, *Come Together: John Lennon in His Time* (New York: Random House, 1990), 182.

6. "John Winston Lennon," FBI Records: The Vault; Wiener, *Gimme Some Truth*.

7. Albin Krebs, "Notes on People," *New York Times*, March 4, 1972.

8. "John Winston Lennon," FBI Records: The Vault; Wiener, *Gimme Some Truth*.

9. David Bird, "Lindsay Deplores Action to Deport Lennons as a 'Grave Injustice,'" *New York Times*, April 29, 1972.

10. "John Winston Lennon," FBI Records: The Vault; Wiener, *Gimme Some Truth*.

11. Lennon, interview by McCabe and Schonfeld, *Tittenhurst Park*.

12. *The U.S. vs. John Lennon*, directed by David Leaf and John Scheinfeld (Paramount, 2006).

13. Douglas Brinkley, *Tour of Duty: John Kerry and the Vietnam War* (New York: William Morrow, 2004), 399–400.

14. Treen, "Justice for a Beatle," *Rolling Stone*.

15. Albin Krebs, "Notes on People: Lennons' Deportation Hearing

Delayed," *New York Times*, May 2, 1972.

16. Editorial, "Love It and Leave It," *New York Times*, May 2, 1972.

CHAPTER 5: WORDPLAY

1. Excerpts from *The Dick Cavett Show* broadcasts of September 11, 24, 1971 and May 11, 1972, copyright © Daphne Productions, Inc., used with permission of Mr. Cavett and Daphne Productions.

2. "John Winston Lennon," FBI Records: The Vault, http://vault.fbi. gov/john-winston-lennon. Additional contextual and background information can be found in Jon Wiener, *Gimme Some Truth: The John Lennon FBI Files* (Berkeley: University of California Press, 2000).

3. Ben Fong-Torres, "Lennon's Song: The Man Can't F**k Our Music," *Rolling Stone*, February 18, 1971.

4. *The Dick Cavett Show*, May 1972.

5. Jon Wiener, *Come Together: John Lennon in His Time* (New York: Random House, 1990), 214.

6. Editorial, "Love It and Leave It," *New York Times*, May 2, 1972.

7. Albin Krebs, "Notes on People," *New York Times*, May 13, 1972.

8. From the book *Talk Show* by Dick Cavett. Copyright © 2009 by Richard A. Cavett. All rights reserved. Reprinted by arrangement with Henry Holt and Company, LLC.

9. Cavett, *Talk Show*, xvi.

10. "Lennon Makes Plea at Close of Hearing," *New York Times*, May 18, 1972.

11. Editorial, "Unhand That Beatle," *Washington Daily News*, May 9, 1972.

12. "John Lennon and Yoko Ono to Have Press Conference," *Rosslyn Review*, May 4, 1972.

13. Ralph J. Gleason, "Perspectives: Fair Play for John and Yoko," *Rolling Stone*, June 22, 1972.

14. Grace Lichtenstein, "John and Yoko: 'If There's Mercy, I'd Like It, Please,'" *New York Times*, May 21, 1972.

15. "John Winston Lennon," FBI Records: The Vault; Wiener, *Gimme Some Truth*.

16. Stephen Holden, "'Que Pasa, New York?' Indeed," *Rolling Stone*, July 20, 1972.

17. Robert Christgau, "John Lennon's Realpolitik," *Newsday*, July 9, 1972.

CHAPTER 6: "WE'LL GET IT RIGHT NEXT TIME"

1. Steven D. Price, *1001 Greatest Things Ever Said about California* (Guilford, CT: Lyons Press/Globe Pequot, 2007), p. 151.

2. Paul Krassner, *Confessions of a Raving, Unconfined Nut: Misadventures in the Counter-Culture* (New York: Touchstone, 1994), 181.

3. John Lennon and Yoko Ono, interview with Geraldo Rivera, WABC-TV *Eyewitness News*, broadcast and unedited footage, recorded August 5, 1972.

4. Sridhar Pappu, "Being Geraldo," *Atlantic*, June 2005.

5. Larry Kane, *Lennon Revealed* (Philadelphia: Running Press, 2005), 242.

6. "John Winston Lennon," FBI Records: The Vault, http://vault.fbi.gov/john-winston-lennon. Additional contextual and background information can be found in Jon Wiener, *Gimme Some Truth: The John Lennon FBI Files* (Berkeley: University of California Press, 2000).

7. Bob Gruen, *John Lennon: The New York Years* (New York: Stewart, Tabori & Chang, 2005), 40.

8. *John Lennon: Live in NYC* (Sony Video, 1986).

9. Toby Mamis, "One to One," *Soul Sounds*, December 1972.

10. David Fricke, review of *Live in New York City* by John Lennon, *Rolling Stone*, April 10, 1986.

CHAPTER 7: "YOU CAN'T KEEP A GOOD BAND DOWN"

1. Pete Hamill, "John Lennon: Long Night's Journey into Day," *Rolling Stone*, June 5, 1975.

2. Roy Carr, "Instant Karma!" *New Musical Express*, October 7, 1972.

3. "Random Notes," *Rolling Stone*, October 26, 1972.

4. Toby Mamis, review of *Elephant's Memory*, *Melody Maker*, December 2, 1972.

5. Richard Nusser, "Riffs," *Village Voice*, October 5, 1972.

6. "Pop Best Bets," *Cash Box*, September 30, 1972.

7. Nick Tosches, review of *Elephant's Memory*, *Rolling Stone*, November 5, 1972.

8. Hamill, *Rolling Stone*.

9. Wiener, *Come Together*, 253.

10. Calliope Kurtz, "The Feminist Songs of Yoko Ono," *Perfect Sound Forever*, May 2007.

11. Bill Dowlding, "em, not just another pretty band," *Milwaukee Bugle-American*, November 8–15, 1972.

12. Lenny Kaye, "Sound Scene," *Cavalier*, December 1972.

13. Nick Tosches, review of *Approximately Infinite Universe* by Yoko Ono, *Rolling Stone*, March 15, 1973.

14. "John Winston Lennon," FBI Records: The Vault; Wiener, *Gimme Some Truth*.

15. Davies, ed., *The John Lennon Letters*, 251.

16. Guiliano, *Lennon in America*, 54.

17. Jon Landau, review of *Mind Games* by John Lennon, *Rolling Stone*, January 3, 1974.

18. Hamill, *Rolling Stone*.

19. Francis Schoenberger, "He Said, She Said," *Spin*, October 1988.

20. Tim Riley, *Lennon: The Man, the Myth, the Music—the Definitive Life* (New York: Hyperion), 2011.

21. Christopher Sandford, *McCartney* (Cambridge, MA: Da Capo Press, 2007), 228.

22. John Lennon, interview with Bob Harris, *The Old Grey Whistle Test*, BBC Radio 2, April 1975.

23. Giuliano, *Lennon in America*, 60.

24. Anthony Fawcett, *John Lennon: One Day at a Time, A Personal Biography of the Seventies* (New York: Grove Press, 1976), 145.

25. Hamill, *Rolling Stone*.

26. Wiener, *Gimme Some Truth*, 283.

SELECT BIBLIOGRAPHY AND FURTHER READING

Brinkley, Brinkley. *Tour of Duty: John Kerry and the Vietnam War.* New York: William Morrow, 2004.

Carson, David A. *Grit, Noise, and Revolution.* Ann Arbor: University of Michigan Press, 2005.

Cavett, Dick. *Talk Show: Confrontations, Pointed Commentary, and Off-Screen Secrets.* New York: Times Books/Henry Holt, 2010.

Coleman Ray. *Lennon: The Definitive Biography.* New York: Harper Perennial, 1992.

Davies, Hunter, ed. *The John Lennon Letters.* New York: Little, Brown and Company, 2012.

Douglas, Mike, with Thomas Kelly and Michael Heaton, *I'll Be Right Back: Memories of TV's Greatest Talk Show*. New York: Simon & Schuster, 2000.

Fawcett, Anthony. *John Lennon: One Day at a Time, A Personal Biography of the Seventies*. New York: Grove Press, 1976.

Giuliano, Geoffrey. *Lennon in America: 1971–1980, Based in Part on the Lost Lennon Diaries*. New York: Cooper Square Press, 2000.

Gruen, Bob. *John Lennon: The New York Years*. New York: Stewart, Tabori & Chang, 2005.

Kane, Larry. *Lennon Revealed*. Philadelphia: Running Press, 2005.

Krassner, Paul. *Confessions of a Raving, Unconfined Nut: Misadventures in the Counterculture*. New York: Touchstone, 1994.

Lennon, John. *Skywriting by Word of Mouth*. New York: HarperCollins, 1986.

McCabe, Peter and Robert D. Schonfeld. *Apple to the Core: The Unmaking of the Beatles* . New York: Pocket Books, 1972.

Norman, Philip. *John Lennon: The Life*. New York: HarperCollins, 2008.

Ono, Yoko, ed. *Memories of John Lennon*. New York: HarperCollins, 2005.

Riley, Tim. *Lennon: The Man, the Myth, the Music—the Definitive Life*. New York: Hyperion, 2011.

Sandford, Christopher. *McCartney*. Cambridge, MA: Da Capo Press, 2007.

Wiener, Jon. *Come Together: John Lennon in His Time*. New York: Random House, 1990.

———. *Gimme Some Truth: The John Lennon FBI Files* (Berkeley: University of California Press, 2000).

INDEX

JAMES A. MITCHELL is the author of *But for the Grace: Profiles in Peace from a Nation at War* (Mansion Field, 2009), the story of an orphanage in Sri Lanka's war-torn northeast; rock biography *It Was All Right: Mitch Ryder's Life in Music* (Wayne State University Press, 2008); and tales from a rural newspaper, *Applegate: Freedom of the Press in a Small Town* (University Press of America, 2002). A reporter and editor for more than thirty years in New York and Michigan, and as a US Army soldier-journalist, Mitchell's works on a wide range of subjects have appeared in publications including *Entertainment Weekly, Crain's Detroit Business, The Humanist, Video Business,* and *Starlog.* From South Asia Mitchell produced video features for CNN's iReport in the aftermath of the twenty-six-year civil war. Mitchell lives in Southeast Michigan.

SEVEN STORIES PRESS is an independent book publisher based in New York City. We publish works of the imagination by such writers as Nelson Algren, Russell Banks, Octavia E. Butler, Ani DiFranco, Assia Djebar, Ariel Dorfman, Coco Fusco, Barry Gifford, Martha Long, Luis Negrón, Hwang Sok-yong, Lee Stringer, and Kurt Vonnegut, to name a few, together with political titles by voices of conscience, including Subhankar Banerjee, the Boston Women's Health Collective, Noam Chomsky, Angela Y. Davis, Human Rights Watch, Derrick Jensen, Ralph Nader, Loretta Napoleoni, Gary Null, Greg Palast, Project Censored, Barbara Seaman, Alice Walker, Gary Webb, and Howard Zinn, among many others. Seven Stories Press believes publishers have a special responsibility to defend free speech and human rights, and to celebrate the gifts of the human imagination, wherever we can. In 2012 we launched Triangle Square books for young readers with strong social justice and narrative components, telling personal stories of courage and commitment. For additional information, visit www.sevenstories.com.